W9-BZL-616

SUCCEED
WITH
MATH

DISCARDED
JENKS LRC
GORDON COLLEGE

Sheila Tobias

SUCCEED WITH MATH

Every Student's Guide to Conquering Math Anxiety

JENKS L.R.C.
GORDON COLLEGE
255 GRAPEVINE RD.
WENHAM, MA 01984-1895

College Entrance Examination Board, New York

QA
11
.T675
1987

In all of its book publishing activities the College Board endeavors to present the works of authors who are well qualified to write with authority on the subject at hand and to present accurate and timely information. However, the opinions, interpretations, and conclusions of the authors are their own and do not necessarily represent those of the College Board; nothing contained herein should be assumed to represent an official position of the College Board or any of its members.

Copies of this book are available from your local bookseller or may be ordered from College Board Publications, Box 886, New York, New York 10101-0886. The price is $12.95.

Editorial inquiries concerning this book should be directed to Editorial Office, The College Board, 45 Columbus Avenue, New York, New York 10023-6992.

Copyright © 1987 by Sheila Tobias. All rights reserved.
Text reproduced in Figure 4, pp. 22–25, is reprinted by permission from *Algebra and Trigonometry* by David Cohen, © 1986 by West Publishing Company. All rights reserved.

The College Board, Scholastic Aptitude Test, SAT, and the acorn logo are registered trademarks of the College Entrance Examination Board.

Library of Congress Catalog Number: 87-072159
ISBN: 0-87447-259-8

Printed in the United States of America

9 8 7 6 5 4 3 2

To my parents, Rose and Paul J. Tobias,
who know the joys of learning and teaching
and passed these on to me.

Contents

I
Getting Math in Focus

1
Making Math Work for You   3

2
Reading Math   15

3
Problem Solving 35

II

▬*Thinking About Mathematics*▬

4

The Wonders of Pi   *57*

5

Taming Numbers   *83*

6

Equalities and Inequalities *113*

III
From School Mathematics to the Real World

7
Social Science:
Researching Sex-Role Attitudes *151*

8
Biology:
Exploring Population Genetics *179*

9

Economics and Business: Planning for Profits 201

10

Getting Comfortable with Math **235**

Acknowledgments

This book, like all of the other major projects of my career, has been a team effort. I like to think of myself as the conductor of a small orchestra made up of talents very different from mine. I provide the melody, much of the score (and most of the percussion). But I could not have written this book, which crosses so many disciplines, without the fine instrumentalists listed below.

Deepest thanks go to my chief research assistant, Laurie Wern, whose competence in mathematics and commitment to teaching will serve her well as she pursues her doctorate in mathematics education at Ohio State. I owe very special thanks to Patricia Mac-Corquodale, Associate Professor of Sociology at the University of Arizona, and Stephen T. Abedon (who doubles as my nephew), candidate for the Ph.D. in microbiology at the same university, for allowing me to use their current projects as case studies demonstrating the power of mathematics.

Assisting with the economics and business chapter were Nancy Williams, who recently graduated with a degree in quantitative economics from Stanford, and Peggy Baranek, a candidate for the Ph.D. in management information systems at the University of Arizona. Readers of that section were Professors Nikki Kravitz and Markita Price of the Business and Computer Science departments, respectively, at Stephens College in Columbia, Missouri. In command of the original graphics was Laurie Weckel, whose ability to translate complex ideas into visuals has made her my frequent collaborator on instructional projects. And when I needed an editor familiar with the learning levels of precollege students, I turned, to my great good fortune, to Ted Feragne, instructor in English at the Salpointe High School in Tucson, who read every page of this manuscript and helped make it more accessible to the reader.

I owe a very special debt to Michael Tangredi, professor of mathematics at St. Benedict's College, who permitted me to borrow for Chapter 6 what I consider to be a very good introductory example for the teaching of linear programming. Dr. Tangredi is currently at work on a college mathematics textbook on linear programming.

My thanks to my various readers: David Gay, Margaret Meyer, and Reuben Hersh, professors of mathematics, respectively, at the universities of Arizona, Wisconsin, and New Mexico; George Marcek, retired instructor in physics at Tucson high schools; Ray Wakeland, a high school science teacher-in-training; Susan B. Auslander, lecturer in mathematics at the State University of New York at Purchase and my collaborator on the Math Anxiety Project; Mark Paulson, instructor in mathematics at Salpointe; and to students Teresa Zimmerman and Nicholas Mansour of Tucson, and Janae Donady of Middletown, Connecticut.

My special thanks to Gloria Stern, my agent, for urging me to take on this assignment, and to Carolyn Trager, my editor at the College Board, for allowing me to take it in a far more ambitious direction than either of us had envisioned at the beginning.

Each of my associates tried valiantly to keep me from errors of fact and of interpretation. I take responsibility for any they missed.

And to Carl: Thanks for feeding me, teaching me, and believing in me (and not in that order).

Tucson, Arizona
September 1987

Foreword

Many of the forces changing today's world are part of the visible facade of public life. Issues such as the population explosion, nuclear policy, information technology, AIDS, and Third World debt are common components of daily news and national policy. But mathematics, the subject of this book, exerts hidden forces that shape and strengthen this facade; mathematics provides an invisible framework that molds the more visible surface features of daily life.

Mathematics is a necessary foundation for most subjects students study at a modern university: natural science, social science, technology, engineering, agriculture, management, business. These and many other disciplines use mathematics in increasingly important ways. Moreover, the increased quantification of public policy issues signals the need for greater mathematical literacy among the educated.

Despite the pervasive nature of mathematics as the power broker in so many important arenas of human activity, it is largely hidden from public view. Those who fear it don't want to think about it; those who escaped from school without it don't want to talk about it; and those who practice it don't want to discuss it in public.

Students preparing for careers in the twenty-first century cannot afford to accept the mathematical myth of their elders—that mathematics is an esoteric elective necessary only for scientific geniuses. Mathematics is important for every career, albeit in different ways and to different degrees. It should be part of everyone's education during every year of study.

The sad fact is that American students study mathematics less intensively than those in most other industrialized countries. To make matters worse, demographic data suggest a rapidly developing crisis in the equality of opportunity to learn. By the year 2000, 30 percent of our nation's youth will be black or Hispanic, yet virtually no black or Hispanic students are currently choosing careers in mathematics or in mathematics education. In 1986 only nine American blacks and Hispanics received doctoral degrees in mathematics, and only a handful of the top 10,000 black and Hispanic college freshmen indicated an interest in majoring in mathematics. Without teachers and leaders well educated in mathematics, black and Hispanic youth will lack the role models necessary to inspire them to master this most fundamental discipline.

The participation of women in the mathematical sciences is somewhat better than it was a quarter century ago but is still far from where it might be. In the last 15 years there has been virtually no change in the number of women who receive advanced degrees in mathematics, even though during this same period increasing numbers of women have attained comparable distinction in many other careers and professions. Indeed, the retention rate of women from bachelor's to master's to doctoral degrees is far worse in mathematics than in any other science.

A few years ago the Alfred P. Sloan Foundation initiated a national program to stimulate what they called "The New Liberal Arts," based on the premise that in this age all educated men and women need thorough grounding in quantitative and technological thinking. Mathematical subjects were once part of the seven classical liberal arts, the studies "appropriate for a free person." Today, as in antiquity, the mathematical sciences are again an essential part of the education required for free men and women.

Yet, the paradox of our times is that as mathematics becomes increasingly powerful, only the powerful seem to benefit from it. The ability to think mathematically—broadly interpreted—is absolutely crucial to advancement in virtually every career. Confidence in dealing with data, skepticism in analyzing arguments, persistence in penetrating complex problems, and literacy in communicating about technical matters are the enabling arts offered by the new mathematical sciences.

The well-being of our nation depends on the ability of our youth to succeed with mathematics. For this to happen we must make mathematics visible by destroying myths, overcoming anxieties, and removing barriers. Once mathematics is out in the open, unencumbered by mystery and obfuscation, fear will diminish and confidence will increase.

Succeed with Math will motivate many students to sustain (or restart) their progress in mathematics. It is an important undertaking with a valuable message for all youth: Don't stop your study of mathematics.

Lynn Arthur Steen
Professor of Mathematics, St. Olaf College
Former President, Mathematical Association of America

Part

I

Getting Math
In
Focus

Chapter

1

Making Math Work for You

There are two myths about mathematics that need to be put to rest. One is that college-level mathematics is too difficult for otherwise intelligent students to master. Another is that without mathematics you can live a productive intellectual and professional life. I don't believe these myths and when you finish this book, you won't either.

You are going to discover some new ways of thinking about mathematics, of reading mathematics, of studying mathematics, of talking the language of mathematics, and of appreciating the power of using mathematics. You will also be taken on a few adventures, first to some of the more interesting ideas in elementary mathematics that you may not have thought about before now, though you had all the requisite equipment. Then, you will get a look at the offices and laboratories where work involving mathematical applications is currently going on. There, at the frontiers of three different fields—social science, population genetics, and business management—you will see for yourself how mathematics has become one of the most important tools of modern life.

Mathematics is no longer just an entry-level prerequisite for engineering, the physical sciences, and statistics. Its principles and techniques, along with computers, have become part of almost all areas of work; and its logic is used in thinking about almost everything. This is a big change from the days when a number of professions were virtually math-free. Today, many occupations that do not require college-level calculus or statistical skills at the outset demand them later on for anyone aiming toward promotion into management or work in more interesting technical areas.

Mathematical expressions like "the slope of the curve," "zero sum," "normalized distribution," and "asymptotic" are no longer just the mutterings of bearded thinkers who cannot remember to wear socks of the same color. They have become part of the basic vocabulary of business, politics, library management, health care, and even social work. One important reason is that mathematical expressions give us a way of thinking about relationships that would otherwise be unavailable to us. Just as your ability to think more complex thoughts was enhanced every time you learned a new word or phrase, so your ability to understand abstract concepts will be enriched when you master mathematical ideas like "limits," "nonlinear," and "exponential growth."

What awaits you in college-level mathematics is an excitement that is inseparable from hard work. The aims of this book are to help you conquer any anxiety you may have about exploring math and to give you the tools to make the subject your own.

Math Anxiety

Where Does It Come From?

Many high school and college students are unwilling to study higher mathematics and science because they are convinced they just can't do math. This idea may have originated early in their elementary schooling when they were given the impression that certain people *can* do math and certain people simply cannot.

I have interviewed hundreds of "math anxious" college students. They can all remember the moment when they began to doubt that they had what it takes to learn math. In some cases, it was because someone had told them girls don't do math, or blacks don't become engineers. Others came to the conclusion that they would either be good with numbers *or* with words, but that they couldn't be good with both. Since our American culture is somewhat ambivalent about mathematicians as role models, some students decided they didn't want to be one. Besides, math seemed dreary, and never any fun.

None of these assumptions are true. First, if there still are few females and blacks in the top tiers of working mathematicians and scientists, it is not because they are genetically inferior, but because there have been social and institutional barriers for them to overcome that are only slowly disappearing. Second, while some writers don't like math and some mathematicians don't like to write, there is no evidence whatsoever that writing ability and mathematics ability are mutually exclusive. On the contrary, college admissions counselors know that the student who shows high capability in *both* the mathematics and verbal sections of the SAT is more likely to succeed in math than the student who has a severely skewed score, strong only in quantitative skills. And, finally, while elementary mathematics may indeed be repetitive, it is a skill that must be practiced if you are to get to the creative part later on.

Another source of trauma for many young people is the *style* of the mathematics classroom. Students complain that there is little opportunity for debate or discussion. Many say they like English and social studies better than math because they can participate more in class and there is not so much pressure to find the one right answer. Mathematics does depend on right answers, but it can also be experienced as a series of discoveries that we all make for ourselves. More often than not, however, math is presented as a fixed set of rules to be digested whole and without dispute, which may discourage students from learning.

"I used to panic so about timed tests," one college student told her math-anxiety counselor, "that the only thing I really learned in all my years of elementary schooling was how to do quick subtraction and short division." This student was forever looking at the clock, counting the minutes she had left for the test, dividing them into the number of questions remaining, and, of course, getting more and more anxious.

Few people can think clearly and well with a clock ticking away. It's hard to perform at the blackboard with thirty sets of eyes watching you. No one likes a subject that is presented rigidly and uncompromisingly. And most people do not do well when they are scared. Some years ago, investigators decided that "math inability" may not be the result of a failure of intellect, but rather of nerve, which led to the establishment of "math-anxiety clinics" around the nation.

How Does Math Anxiety Work?

It will be easier to understand why math anxiety occurs if you think of your brain as a three-part system with an input area, a memory bank, and some kind of understanding and recall pathways connecting the two. (This hypothetical model of the brain is useful for thinking about math anxiety.)

Figure 1

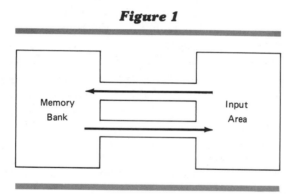

If the system is working well, when you look at a math problem or a new piece of mathematical information you will call up from memory the right formula or approach. You will move back and forth effortlessly along the recall and understanding pathways of your brain until you succeed in solving the problem or in understanding the new mathematical idea. Anytime you get stuck, you will return to your memory bank, or get some more input from the problem, or refer to your textbook. Perhaps you will draw a diagram or two. Or you will put some hypothetical numbers into the problem to make it more concrete. But whatever you do, you will be *busy* moving along the pathways of your brain, activating your memory, using your analytic skills, learning and doing.

Now, suppose your memory bank is intact and your understanding and recall skills are well developed, but every time you look at some new mathematical material or problem, your emotions come into play. You panic. You tell yourself: "This is just the kind of problem I can never solve." You feel the tension that comes from time pressure or the uncertainty that comes from lack of confidence. What might your brain system look like then?

Figure 2

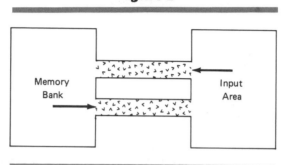

The understanding and recall pathways have become cluttered by emotions. There is an inability to think, but not because the "hardware" is inadequate. The input, memory, and understanding and recall systems are just as good as they were before. But, because the pathways have been blocked, you cannot remember. You lose self-confidence because you don't seem able to analyze the problem. You may even doubt that you have the intelligence to do the job. But, in truth, the only reason you cannot work is that your feelings have created too much "static" in your brain. Soon, your pencil stops moving. Your brain stops functioning. You can't work, you assume, because you can't think. But in fact, it's just the reverse: you can't think because you have stopped working.

Getting Over Math Anxiety

Active Thinking

"Thinking" in mathematics involves working. Did you ever notice that your math teacher can hardly talk to you about mathematics without writing on the chalkboard or on a piece of paper? There are stories about mathematicians dining together who fill up their napkins (and sometimes even the tablecloth) with calculations, diagrams, and drawings while talking about their work.

They know something you don't—that only by trying new avenues of thought, putting down first one idea and then another, turning a diagram over and over in your mind, doing calculations or checking procedures, can you learn and solve problems. Your emotions have made you stop; the essence of doing math is to *keep going*.

Self-Monitoring

To reduce math anxiety, you must learn first to recognize when panic starts, then to identify the static in your analytic and retrieval systems, and, finally, to clear up the static without ceasing to work on the problem as you work on yourself.

How can you do all this at once? The essence of math-anxiety

Figure 3

My feelings – Thoughts	My work

therapy is self-monitoring. You can practice this while doing home-work or studying. Draw a line down the center of a piece of paper. On one side of the page record your feelings and thoughts, however random and seemingly disconnected they may be. On the other side of the page keep your notes, calculations, or problem-solving steps.

You may not be able to capture elusive feelings and thoughts the first time you try this exercise. But in time you will find that you have learned to observe your own "self-statements"—what you say to yourself when under stress. This is one way to discover what obstacles you may be creating for yourself when you work at math. Then you can begin to get rid of the emotional static that prevents your success.

Suppose you wrote, as so many math-anxious students do, "This is just the kind of problem I could never solve." The next step would be to ask yourself: "What is making this problem diffi-cult for me, and what can I do to make it easier?"

Giving Yourself Permission

The point of the divided-page exercise is to learn to give your-self permission to explore your own confusion and to find out what is making the problem or the new material seem difficult. As you become more and more familiar with your own learning style, you will become more adept at discovering flaws. More important, the exercise permits you to keep working.

Perhaps you have recognized the real purpose of the divided-page exercise already: when you are stuck and not able to put anything down on the right-hand side of your page, you can still be writing your thoughts and feelings on the left. That means you can continue working, even if you aren't doing math calculations. You will be writing notes to yourself when you are unable to write a solution to an equation. You will be writing comments when you can't figure out the calculation. But you will be working all the while, thinking about the problem by thinking about why you are having trouble with it, clearing the static from your mind, reviving your analytic powers as you observe yourself at work.

Soon, your ability to analyze your own problems will become a source of insight into the math problem. In time, the two mental activities will become so entwined that you won't be able to say with certainty whether the insight that finally gave you a way to crack the problem came from the problem itself or from your own assessment of its difficulties.

Here's an example of the divided-page handling of a problem:

A car is driven 50,000 miles. Its five tires (one is the spare) are rotated regularly and frequently. How many miles will any one tire have traveled on the road by the end of the trip?

On the left-hand side of the page, one student writes: "I know there's a formula for this problem. I even think I once knew it. But I've forgotten it and I don't think I can solve the problem without the formula. So, what to do? Let's draw a diagram, construct a table, plug in some numbers. Maybe the formula will pop up." It did.

And another: "I keep coming up with 10,000 miles (50,000 ÷ 5 = 10,000), but I know that's wrong because the total mileage is too small for a tire to have traveled on that trip. Perhaps that's the answer to another question. I am always better at coming up with questions than with answers. What could that other question be?"

And, "What's confusing me is the word 'rotated.' A car goes 50,000 miles. If the driver rotates all five tires, including the spare, 'rotated' seems to have two meanings: 'turning on the road' and 'changing position on the car.' Could it mean both? Perhaps my first task is to figure out how five tires get their positions changed so that each one is on the road an equal number of miles. And, how are 'regularly' and 'frequently' to be understood?" (See further discussion of this problem on p. 47.)

Self-Mastery

At this point, the extra time it takes to fill up the left-hand side of the divided page begins to pay off. Writing things down frees you from the almost paralyzing effort of staring at a hard problem or a page of confusing text. Because thinking in mathematics involves doing, writing down random feelings and thoughts breaks the tension and the sense of isolation. You are at least "talking" constructively to yourself. At its best, the divided page provides a way to tune in to your intuition and common sense.

Best of all, the tuning-in process teaches you about your own idiosyncrasies in learning about and solving math problems. Some students don't feel secure until they have drawn something. So much the better. Draw something. Others need to rephrase the question in their own words. Do it. Still others want to put numbers into long, abstract mathematical statements or just to talk themselves through a procedure.

In talking with students who are successful in math, I found that they are not necessarily smarter than the rest of us, but they know themselves very well. They can anticipate the difficulties they are going to have. They know what kinds of questions and actions will give them the power and confidence to continue. They know when to skim and when to focus in on a paragraph, sometimes for hours at a time. They are never bored because they are busy. They never quit because they recognized long ago that progress in mathematics involves making just a little headway, one step at a time. They don't judge themselves as harshly as we judge ourselves when answer don't come out right. They are patient, tenacious, and rarely very fast.

══════*Another Way of Looking*══════
at Math Competence

If I could pass one new "law" in the teaching of mathematics, it would be to have students graded on (1) how well they approach a problem to be solved; (2) how many different ways they can solve the problem; and (3) how thoughtful an essay they can write about what makes a particular problem mathematically interesting. It is in thinking about a problem before and after it's been solved that much mathematical imagination can be brought into play. And it is imagination, in the form of intuition and interesting analogies, that is the source of invention in math.

It is not surprising that many students do not learn the importance of imagination. An algebra textbook states a problem and immediately refers to the relevant formula. Textbook authors and teachers don't talk to students about *their* many trials and errors the first time they look at certain problems, or about how much mathematics they learn in the course of the struggle itself. We get the impression that they can do math instantly and with ease. It would help to know more specifically how math experts cope with problems and what they do when they forget what to do. Those insights might reveal the skills really needed in mathematics: the ability and the courage—both are equally important—to figure things out for oneself.

Looking Ahead

No single book can transform anxiety or indifference into unbridled enthusiasm. My goal is more modest. The reverse of math anxiety, I decided long ago, is not expertise in mathematics; it is "math mental health," which I define as the willingness to learn the math you need when you need it.

This is not a conventional math book. Mathematics, the practitioners will tell you, is something you *do,* not something you read about. But, on the way to math mental health you may need a preview to gain a sense, if not mastery, of what lies ahead. Since mathematics is cumulative, the curriculum in elementary school and junior and senior high school moves systematically from one concept to the next in logical order, building on what has gone before. But if, along the way, you have lost confidence about mathematics and no longer enjoy it, you may need a tour such as this one, which looks at what you already know and points toward what is to come, to rekindle your enthusiasm.

To take one example that is developed in some detail in Chapter 4, pi was presented to you in seventh grade as a kind of utensil with which you would be able to solve many new kinds of problems. You were not expected to *understand* pi in any serious way, just to use it. In this book you will be able to explore the wonders of pi and learn about its significance both in the history of mathematical thinking and in its many applications, but you won't be asked to solve any circumference and area problems with it.

Mathematicians have struggled for centuries not simply to find answers to questions but to figure out which questions they should be asking. Questions about infinities, a topic mentioned in Chapter 5, didn't arise until approximately two hundred years ago. The *idea* that there is more than one infinity is an interesting and important one, but there is no need, the first time you consider multiple infinities, to learn the reasoning behind Cantor's discovery of them. What matters at that point is seeing the range of what lies ahead and behind the set of tools that mathematicians have made available.

During the Renaissance, there were math "duels" between people who had figured out a formula or way of solving a problem that they kept secret from one another. Mathematics is no longer a secret code, nor is it a set of magical pronouncements meant to mystify you. It is full of utilities that no one would have dreamed of until recently. In Chapters 7, 8, and 9 your tour of mathematics will take you to some workshops where mathematics techniques are in daily use, and you will be shown how very empowering those methods are.

If you are to become a capable user of mathematics, you will need to *do* math: to solve problems; to use notation; to comprehend the principles behind the techniques. But for now, you will benefit from having a peek at some of the ideas in mathematics that I, as a previous math avoider, have come to find interesting and important.

Each of the chapters in this book is self-contained, which means you don't have to read them in any particular order. If you are primarily interested in mathematical applications, you might want to start with Part III. If you want to know a little bit more about some familiar mathematics, you might want to begin with the wonders of pi, or explore numbers and inequalities (Chapters 4, 5, and 6). If your problem has been reading math, Chapter 2 is where you might begin. If you have not developed reliable techniques for problem solving, you might want to look at Chapter 3. The Further Reading section suggests some sources to go to next if you are interested in any particular stopping place on this tour. The main purpose of this book is not to teach you math but, rather, to make you want to learn it.

Do you have to *think* like a mathematician in order to *do* math? I doubt it. If you can derive the formulas you have to work with, of course, you will feel more secure. (You won't forget something once you have figured it out for yourself.) If you can make connections among mathematical principles, you will have a better grasp of the whole. As you go along, you will inevitably develop a sense of awe, for mathematics is a wondrous way of imposing order on the universe. Remember, it took thousands of years for the very best minds, working overtime, to create the formulas ordinary college students are learning today. That legacy should not be a burden to us, but should be taken for what it is: a gift! And, above all, it should be taken, not avoided or left unexplored.

Chapter

2

Reading Math

When students pick up a mathematics text and have trouble following it, they often conclude that they just can't do math. However, the problem may not be the math itself as much as not understanding how to approach the text.

Reading a mathematics text is not like reading any other kind of book. In books on other subjects, clarity often is achieved through repetition: using different words to restate a single idea; slowing the pace; using a spiral kind of organization that keeps coming back to the same idea at different levels; using topic and summary sentences to nail down what the paragraph contains; and foreshadowing the points to be made later on. Introductory and concluding sections are always helpful to the reader.

Now, imagine pages of text that allow for virtually no repetition, no varying of pace, few topic and concluding sentences, as few words as possible, written with the expectation that you will not proceed to the next sentence or point without having thoroughly mastered the previous one. That's the kind of writing you will encounter in mathematics texts.

It is not that the author wants to keep you in the dark. On the contrary, the book was designed as a teaching device, but until you understand how you are supposed to read a math text, you will not get out of it what you should.

First, in mathematical writing clarification is achieved by constructing very precise sentences without any extra words. To the

15

mathematical writer, words or phrases beyond the minimum needed to convey a particular idea may get in the way and confuse instead of clarify.

When you "read" math, then, you have to slow your pace. You have to absorb each word of every sentence. Since important points are not likely to be repeated, it is imperative to go over each sentence several times until the meaning is completely clear.

Second, a mathematics text contains diagrams and other kinds of illustrative material that you must not skim. You must study all tables and graphs carefully. At the beginning you may have trouble trying to read a diagram, to take it apart visually to figure out its meaning. In the examples that follow, you will see how one student makes sense of a math textbook. This may help you find a technique of your own.

Third, every math text includes examples that illustrate the words. Those examples are meant to be worked out, because you will understand the information better if you use it.

Writing as You Read

Mathematics textbook authors and teachers tend to assume that students will read their textbooks with pencil in hand—that they will go back and forth between the text, the illustrations, the examples, and even look ahead to the homework problems, as they read. Properly done, reading mathematics is an activity that involves the reader. The meaning of a page of mathematical writing is only partially given by the text. The rest of the meaning has to be created by you. The problem is that no one may have taught you how to do this.

Kit Building

Kit building is an activity that illustrates one new way to approach mathematical writing. Even if you have never constructed anything from a kit, you can well imagine how you would read the instructions that come with one. After a swift scan of the entire instruction booklet to make sure you have all the necessary parts and tools, you would begin working as you read because the instruction booklet makes little sense until you start putting the pieces together.

The instruction booklet alone (or the software manual if you are trying to learn a new system on your computer) is insufficient. You must continually try out each new step or procedure. The instruction sheet gets you going, but it is in the figuring out and doing that the real learning takes place. That's true not only when building a model or mastering a new computer program, but also when learning mathematics or science. What you have created in the kit-building activity is a three-way relationship between you, the thing you are working on, and what you are reading. If you and the instruction booklet were alone, without the object to work on as you read, not much would really be understood. You can think of a laboratory-science course as a kit-building kind of learning experience. The chemistry or physics laboratory manual is an instruction booklet that gives the details of the experiments you are to set up and monitor. To get the most out of reading your math textbook you are going to have to invent some helpful activities to do as you read.

Reading Equals Activity

Experienced students of mathematics create tasks for themselves as they read a mathematics text. After reading an example, they cover it up and try to reconstruct it from memory. They try to think of other examples that would fit the idea being discussed. They work out the illustrative problems. They think of other relevant problems and try to solve them. In short, they treat reading math as an activity in which they are going to participate almost as much as the writer did in preparing the text.

═══════ Styles of Reading Math ═══════

Reading Down

Reading down is one way to approach a math text. The indented sentences that follow could have been taken from any mathematics textbook currently in use.

Proportions
Ratios are particularly useful in solving many consumer prob-
lems and also problems in science and business.

Stop and consider this sentence. It is meant to introduce the subject
of the math problems to be dealt with later. We don't have to spend
much time deciphering it since there is nothing to be done with it.
The next sentence, however, needs more careful attention.

Especially useful will be the case where we have two ratios set
equal to each other.

This sentence may be more difficult to fathom. It cannot be understood at all unless we understand key terms like *ratios* and *set equal*
to each other. It would be a good idea to stop at this point and try
to think of some examples of two ratios set equal to each other. If
you remember that ratios are often expressed as fractions you might
think of some.

$$\frac{2}{3} = \frac{4}{6}$$

What if you cannot think of an example? Perhaps you don't understand *ratio* or *set equal to* well enough to get anything out of this
section, in which case you should go back right away and clear up
those terms. Or, you might be willing to read on, hoping the following sentences will jog your memory. But realize, if you do this, that
you are taking a risk. You may not be able to go on until you return
to earlier sections in the text or get help from a teacher or friend
or any of the mathematical dictionaries and encyclopedias available
for this purpose. (See the Further Reading section for a list of ready
references.)

The textbook might continue:

Whenever we have this equality between two ratios, we say we
have a proportion.

If you jotted down some examples after reading the previous sentence, all you have to do now is stop and look over your examples
to see for yourself what a proportion really is. To test your understanding, you might ask yourself:

- Can a proportion exist among three ratios? Yes.

$$\frac{1}{2} = \frac{2}{4} = \frac{3}{6}$$

- Can a proportion exist if its ratios are themselves ratios? Yes.

$$\frac{\frac{1}{2}}{1} = \frac{\frac{1}{4}}{\frac{1}{2}}$$

The next sentence in this hypothetical text gives an important new piece of information:

There are four members in a proportion, and if any three of them are known, it is possible to find the missing member.

Here is a new word, "member." We know that member means a part of a group or organization. Is the word being used in that way here?

You should not be discouraged at this point if reading just a few sentences in a math text seems to involve so much work. A little extra work while reading improves your understanding of the material and also saves work later on. If you dissect math sentences this way, perhaps even read them aloud and with a friend to get at all the nuances and to avoid possible misunderstandings, you will be able to proceed step by step through the activities of solving a math problem.

Reading Up

"Reading down" goes from an overview of the subject to the examples and the problems, following the sequence in the textbook. Yet, many good math students report that they do not read their texts this way but instead "read up." Rather than starting with the narrative, they begin by looking at the mathematics itself: the examples, the sample problems, and the solutions to the problem sets.

Suppose we had completely skipped the narrative part of the text discussed previously and had proceeded directly to the examples. Try to verbalize the following example:

$$\frac{2}{a} = \frac{4}{7}.$$

Now look at the sample solution and try to see where the author is attempting to take you:

$$4a = 14$$
$$a = \frac{14}{4} \quad \text{Simplifying}$$
$$a = \frac{7}{2} \quad \text{Dividing the numerator and the denominator by 2.}$$

Ask yourself why the author did each of these steps. If you cannot answer these questions, you should go back to the text and read the material until you find the sentence that clarifies this. Then you can go on with the next sample problem.

A variation of this technique is to start with the homework, the problems themselves. Let's face it, the only way you and your teacher can be certain you have mastered the mathematical principles presented is by how well (or poorly) you do the problems. Some students of mathematics *start* with the problems, try to work them out on the basis of what they know already, and only when they encounter difficulty do they go back to the descriptive sentences in the text. In other words, *they do not read any more of the text than they absolutely have to* in order to make sense of each problem. They are not "reading" the math book at all. They are using the text as a reference, like a dictionary or an encyclopedia. They are certainly not treating the text as if it were a story!

Many of you will find that reading down is the way you generally prefer to tackle a math text. Others may want to read up. It is useful to master both styles so that you can use the one that works best in a particular lesson. Some units in mathematics contain so much new information and describe so many new techniques that it is nearly impossible to start with the examples or the homework problems until you have digested all of the introductory material. As you get more and more skilled in these reading styles, you will probably find yourself reading back and forth, that is, skipping (not skimming) between the text and the problems.

Marking Up a Math Text

Marking up math texts has a long tradition. One of the most famous marginal notes in the history of mathematics was penned by Pierre Fermat, a seventeenth-century French mathematician. Coming upon an unproved statement in a mathematics book, Fermat wrote in the margin of the text: "I have discovered a truly remarkable proof, but this margin is too small to contain it." Fermat died before he could put his proof to paper, but because he had indicated that it could be done, other mathematicians set about trying to prove the statement. The problem, called "Fermat's last theorem," has never been solved. But in the search for a proof, a great deal of important work in the theory of numbers was accomplished that might never have been done if mathematicians had not tried to figure out what Fermat had in mind when he wrote that note.

No matter which way you read a text it is important to write notes, either in the margins (if the textbook is your property) or in your notebook. On the following pages are examples of the thoughtful comments and questions that one mathematics student wrote to herself as she read a textbook. Notice how involved she was in making sense of the material; how she sought examples and continually tested her understanding of what she was reviewing. She was both subject and object of her reading, kit and kit builder in one.

Notice the care with which this reader followed the argument, how she paid attention to definitions, tried to put in numbers and examples of her own. By jotting down her questions and comments she was able to grasp the text. By the time she finished, she had made the material her own.

Just as the divided-page exercise is important as a way of gaining control over your feelings, making detailed notes is important in mastering your understanding of new material.

Figure 4

Slope

Figures 1(a) and (b) below show two straight lines, both of which pass through a given point (2, 1). In what way *Qualitative vs.* do the lines differ from one another? Qualitatively, it's easy to *Quantitative?* see that the line in Figure 1(b) slants upward more sharply than the line in Figure 1(a). To make this idea of slant or direction of a line quantitative, we define a number called the *slope* of a line as follows.

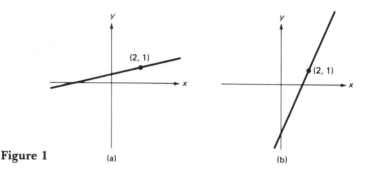

Figure 1   (a)   (b)

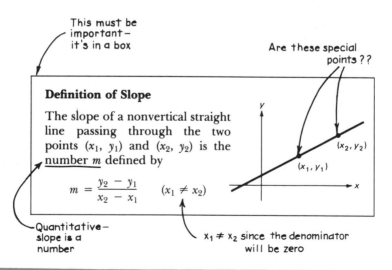

This must be
important —
it's in a box

Are these special
points ? ?

Definition of Slope

The slope of a nonvertical straight line passing through the two points (x_1, y_1) and (x_2, y_2) is the number m defined by

$$m = \frac{y_2 - y_1}{x_2 - x_1} \qquad (x_1 \neq x_2)$$

(x_2, y_2)

(x_1, y_1)

Quantitative —
slope is a
number

$x_1 \neq x_2$ since the denominator
will be zero

Figure 4 continued

Note that the quantity $x_2 - x_1$ appearing in the definition of slope is the amount by which x changes as we move from (x_1,y_1) to (x_2,y_2) along the line. We denote this change in x by the symbol Δx (read *delta x*). Thus $\Delta x = x_2 - x_1$. See Figure 2. Similarly, the symbol Δy is defined to mean the change in y: $\Delta y = y_2 - y_1$. Using these ideas, we can rewrite our definition of slope as $m = \Delta y/\Delta x$.

So m is a ratio of the change in y divided by the change in x

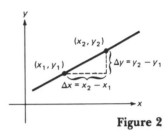

Figure 2

Great! An example

Example 1   Compute the slope of the line in Figure 3.

My question, too

Solution   We use the formula $m = \dfrac{y_2 - y_1}{x_2 - x_1}$. Which point will serve as (x_1,y_1) and which as (x_2,y_2)? It will turn out not to matter how we label our points. Using $(-2,1)$ as (x_1,y_1) and $(4,2)$ as (x_2,y_2), we find $m = \dfrac{2 - 1}{4 - (-2)} = \dfrac{1}{6}$. If instead we use $(4,2)$ as (x_1,y_1) and $(-2,1)$ as (x_2,y_2), we find $m = \dfrac{1 - 2}{-2 - 4} = \dfrac{1}{6}$, the same result. This is not accidental, because in general $\dfrac{y_2 - y_1}{x_2 - x_1} = \dfrac{y_1 - y_2}{x_1 - x_2}$.

So no matter which point I choose as (x_1, y_1), (x_2, y_2) I'll still arrive at the right answer.

I see why: $\dfrac{-1}{-1} = 1$

Figure 3

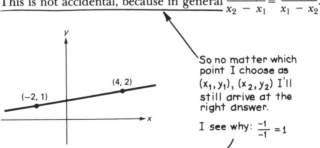

Reason: $\dfrac{y_2 - y_1}{x_2 - x_1} = \dfrac{-1(y_2 - y_1)}{-1(x_2 - x_1)} = \dfrac{-y_2 + y_1}{-x_2 + x_1} = \dfrac{y_1 - y_2}{x_1 - x_2}$

Figure 4 continued

Let us also compute Δx and Δy for the two points given in Figure 3. If we begin at the point $(-2,1)$ and move up the line to $(4,2)$, then we have

$$\Delta x = 4 - (-2) = 6 \text{ and } \Delta y = 2 - 1 = 1$$

Thus $m = \Delta y/\Delta x = 1/6$, as we obtained in Example 1. Note that if instead we start from the point $(4,2)$ and move down the line to $(-2,1)$, then

$$\Delta x = -2 - 4 = -6 \text{ and } \Delta y = 1 - 2 = -1$$

This signals me to pay attention.

Thus $m = \Delta y/\Delta x = -1/-6 = 1/6$, the same result as before, even though Δy and Δx each differ by a sign from their previous values. In summary, the individual values of Δx and Δy depend on which direction you move along the given line. However, the value obtained for the slope $\Delta y/\Delta x$ is the same in both cases.

Example 2   Calculate the slope of the line in Figure 4, first using the points $(2,1)$ and $(3,3)$ and then using $(4,5)$ and $(7,11)$.

Solution   Using the points $(2,1)$ and $(3,3)$, we have $m = \dfrac{3-1}{3-2} = \dfrac{2}{1} = 2$.

Using the points $(4,5)$ and $(7,11)$, we have $m = \dfrac{11-5}{7-4} = \dfrac{6}{3} = 2$.

Note that the two results are the same.

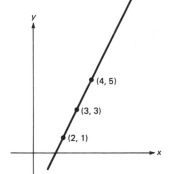

Oh good – this example should answer my question: Does it matter which points I choose on the line ?

Figure 4

The point of Example 2 is to show you that the value obtained for the slope of a given line does not depend on which two points on the line are used to calculate the slope. To demonstrate this is true in general, consider Figure 5.

Figure 4 continued

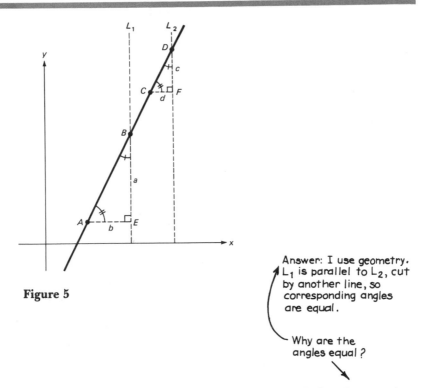

Figure 5

Answer: I use geometry.
L_1 is parallel to L_2, cut
by another line, so
corresponding angles
are equal.

Why are the
angles equal?

The two right triangles in the figure are similar (because the corresponding angles are equal). This implies that the corresponding sides of the two triangles are proportional, and so we have

$$\frac{a}{b} = \frac{c}{d}$$

Now just notice that the left-hand side of this equation represents the slope $\Delta y/\Delta x$ calculated using the points A and B, whereas the right-hand side represents the slope calculated using the points C and D. Thus the values we obtain for the slope are indeed equal.

Now — Try some exercises. . . .

What to Expect in a Math Textbook

In addition to explanatory text and problems to solve, math books contain definitions, derivations, proofs, graphs, equations and other mathematical expressions, and worked-out problems.

Definitions

Definitions are often presented in boldface type or in boxes. The symbol ≡ is sometimes used to indicate that an equivalence is true by definition, as in the mathematical statement

$$X^0 \equiv 1.$$

What gives students difficulty in dealing with definitions is not what is on the page, but what is not. Unaccustomed to axioms, some students spin their wheels (and make themselves unnecessarily anxious) trying to find out what the definition *means* or *where* it comes from or *why* it works. Keep in mind that a definition is simply a way of naming something. Recognize a definition for what it is and don't read too much into it, and you won't get bogged down in material your teacher expects you to accept and move through quickly.

Derivations

Each section of a math book usually has at least one derivation—a form of mathematics that "derives" a formula from math you already know. The derivation shows where the formula comes from, mathematically speaking. You will probably find derivations for all of the important formulas in each math section, particularly when the formulas are new.

The importance of derivations depends to some extent on your teacher and the degree of sophistication of the course. Some teachers will hold you responsible for derivations, others will not. (It is wise to ask in advance what the policy is.) But derivations are useful, whether they are required or not. The derivation will give you a fuller understanding of the formula you are going to use in solving problems. Read the derivation with pencil and paper in hand. Write it out as you go along to follow the reasoning, but do not merely copy what you see in the book. As you write, try to reconstruct the logic for each step. Above all, see if you can locate the essential argument you need to understand if you are to grasp the derivation as a whole. Then, to see if you really understand the derivation, close the book and try to write it out on your own.

Proofs

Proofs are very important in mathematics. You cannot prove a point in mathematics by generating lots of examples, because there is an infinite number of examples and you could never prove your theorem for every one of them. Thus, mathematicians prefer a logical argument to the kind of evidence used in other subjects. In terms of argument, proofs are very much like derivations except for format. In a derivation, the formula you are deriving comes at the end; in a proof, it comes at the beginning.

Derivation: Find the formula for the area of a rectangle.

Proof: Prove that the formula for the area of a rectangle is length times width.

The logic is the same, but the purpose is different. Textbooks vary in whether they are "formula," "theorem," "derivation," or "proof" oriented. It may take some time to get used to the style and flow of logic of the book you are assigned. Be patient with yourself. Study your proofs as you study your derivations, writing them out line by line. Before leaving a proof, see if you can reproduce it—at least its logic—with your book closed.

Graphs

There are three main kinds of illustrations in mathematics texts: graphs, geometrical drawings, and sketches for problems. By far the most important are graphs, particularly the graphing of equations. By the time you start college mathematics, you should be familiar with the principles of Cartesian geometry: the techniques for finding slopes and intercepts should be yours and you should have some skill in plotting linear equations. It is very useful to know how geometric points are represented by a set of numbers and that a particular set of numbers can be represented by a set of geometric points. The power of analytic geometry is great, as you will see in Chapter 6.

To understand graphs and much of the material you will encounter in quantitative subjects other than pure mathematics, it's important to recognize the distinction—represented on graphs—between independent and dependent variables.

When you see an equation in the form

$$y = 3x + 7$$

you should understand that the value of y is *dependent* on the value of x. If x becomes 5, then y becomes 22; if x becomes 500, then y becomes 1,507. Sure, you will say, if y changes, x changes, too. But by convention, the y variable (plotted on the vertical axis) is the dependent variable; the x variable (plotted on the horizontal axis) the independent one. (Only in economics is this done in the reverse as you will see in Chapter 9.)

When reading a Cartesian graph, it is very important to note carefully which quantity is being plotted on the x (independent) axis and which on the y (dependent) axis. This will tell you—even if you have difficulty with the accompanying text—that a change in x is having a corresponding effect on the value of y.

Do not let the *position* of the y variable lead you astray. Just because in

$$y = 3x + 7$$

y stands alone, it is not independent in the mathematical sense of the term. That role is assigned to the x variable along the horizontal axis. And, do not expect all dependent variables to be labeled y and all independent variables to be labeled x. Relationships in physics between time and distance would be labeled t and $s;$ interest rate and monthly payment (in business) might be labeled i and p. The important thing in reading or in creating graphs is that *you* know which variable is independent, which variable is dependent, and that you plot these appropriately on the x and y axes.

Even a simple graph of, say, marriage rates, which is not algebraic in its essence, will follow this convention (see Figure 5). Although the year (the value along the x-axis) is not *causing* the

Figure 5. Americans' Median Age at First Marriage

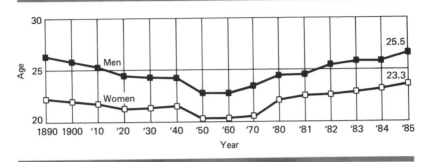

Source: U.S. Census Bureau

increase and decrease in the age of marriage, it is the year that the data collector is changing as the different marriage ages are generated on the *y*-axis.

Pay special attention to any words or numbers on the graphs in a textbook and read captions carefully. Be sure to read the *labels* on the two axes since these tell you what the graph is about. Try to figure out, as you study the graph, what the quantities *mean* in light of what the graph represents.

Finally, pay particular attention to the scale of the graph or diagram. Differences in scale, as shown in Figures 6 and 7, can make the same graph look very different. In Figure 6, the distance

Figure 6

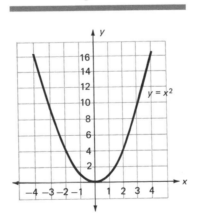

Figure 7

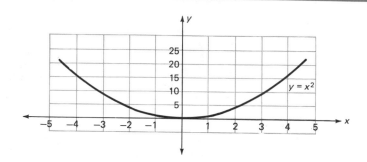

between points on the *x*-axis is small and the curve looks rather narrow. In Figure 7, the distance between points on the *x*-axis is wider, which makes the curve look broad. Yet it is the same "function," that is, relationship, on both graphs that is being plotted: $y = x^2$.

Mathematical Expressions

As you take higher-level mathematics courses your textbooks will be full of mathematical expressions. These expressions will be made up of some familiar elements, like numbers, letters, and the arithmetical operations signs like + and −. They will also include parentheses and brackets to show which operations are to be done and in which order. In addition to these more familiar symbols, you will learn some new notation that very often borrows from the letters of the Greek alphabet and sometimes even from the Hebrew alphabet. The notations speak volumes to people who understand them. It takes practice to gain the understanding of them, but you'll find the results worth the effort.

A mathematical expression can be thought of as a kind of code that communicates directly, not by means of translation. As you read through this book, you will discover for yourself how awkward it is to "translate" mathematical expressions and equations into words (although I do this for you as much as I can). Mathematical expressions are much more efficient and precise statements of what is true and of what you are supposed to do than words.

It is helpful to try to interpret a mathematical statement in words. But as the mathematical material becomes more complex, you have to be sure that your words are at an appropriate level of abstraction. Take the following expression:

$$\frac{\$120}{40} = \$3.$$

At this level, you can state in words that if 40 identical items together cost $120, then any one of those 40 items (any one in the denominator) must cost $3. Dividing the numerator by the denominator gives you the cost (or value) of any one of the items expressed in the denominator. But, when you have a fraction like a/n, where neither a nor n is expressible in numbers, the notation itself should begin to have meaning. If you continued to translate mathematical expressions into arithmetic language, what would you do if you encountered a mathematical statement like this?

$$\frac{(a - V)v}{aTv - RT}$$

Remember, mathematicians are able to *think* in mathematical notation. They rarely translate these expressions any more than advanced foreign-language students translate into their native tongue once they have become fluent. Your aim should be to become fluent in mathematical notation as quickly as you can.

The most common symbols in mathematics are numbers. But letters are symbols, too: those at the end of the alphabet, representing variables—x, y, and z, for example. You may also have noticed that letters at the beginning of the alphabet tend to represent constants, as the term b in the equation below.

$$y = mx + b$$

In addition to these, other letters of the Roman alphabet have been given special meanings, sometimes more than one, such as:

k = constant
i = index, or imaginary number ($\sqrt{-1}$)
e = 2.1718 . . . (a kind of irrational number like pi)
m = slope

These are conventions that people in the field are familiar with and use.

A number of Greek letters also have designated meanings, such as π for the ratio of the circumference of a circle to its diameter, Σ for summing a series of terms, Δ for change in a variable, and so on. Often these letters are combined, as in Δh (signifying change in height), and treated as single terms. You will see trigonometry functions such as sin 60° and tan 10°, and log 1.729 treated as single terms.

You are not expected to memorize these alphabets, but it is useful to learn to *pronounce* all new terms so you can express them comfortably and use them when asking questions. Whenever they are introduced, whether in your text or in class, a full explanation will be given. But it does pay to walk yourself carefully through any equation, noting the terms and the operations that you are going to have to use.

As you take more advanced courses, you will find subscripts and superscripts used more and more frequently. You have already learned that the superscript 2 in x^2 means x is multiplied by itself. The subscript 1 in x_1 is a way of creating more symbols of a similar nature. Just as x and y are different, so x_1 and x_2 are different, too. The superscript is an exponent, an operating symbol; the subscript is more like a proper name, identifying this particular x as different from all others. The more advanced the mathematics, the more complicated the subscripts and superscripts.

The key to success is to take your time, pull the expression apart, and ask questions. Get used to writing out mathematical expressions and make sure you have not left anything out. In short, take the new code you are learning seriously. Even though mathematics is not technically a foreign language, study its "vocabulary," its "grammar," and its "idioms" as if it were.

How Much Studying Is Enough?

How can you tell when you have studied enough? How do you know if you have gone over a chapter as many times as you need to? First, it is a very good sign if you are getting the right answers to most of the problems, and if you understand what is going wrong with those you miss. Second, notice your feelings as you work. If you are alert and confident, chances are you have mastered most of the material. Third, look back over the section on which you have been working. If it all looks easy now and you wonder why you had so much trouble at first, you have succeeded.

Some Problems and Suggestions

If you're not getting the right answers, don't feel clearheaded, and don't find the material easy, try to diagnose precisely what your problem might be so that you can take additional steps. One of the following might describe your situation. If so, try the suggestion given.

Problem: You can't understand the material as it is written in the textbook even after going over the sentences many times.

Suggestion: Try "reading up," or go to another text.

Problem: You read and think you understand. But when you turn to the homework problems you discover that you didn't understand the material after all. This may be because the text is giving you rules and generalizations but not the details you need to do the problems.

Suggestion: First, look back at the general rules and relate various parts of those rules to the parts of the problem you don't understand. Then ask for help. When you go for help, be prepared to ask specific questions. Bring along your attempted work and keep the pencil in *your* hand during the tutoring session. This is a good general rule for all subjects, because if the tutor is doing the writing, then the tutor is doing the thinking.

Problem: You read, complete the homework problems, do all right on the quizzes, but you cannot seem to integrate all of the bits and pieces you learned when preparing for a midterm or a final exam.

Suggestion: You may have to alter the way you do your homework. You may want to schedule one study session to review the lesson passed, one to learn the current lesson, and one to preview the upcoming one. Good math students prepare for exams by redoing problems—not just *some* of them, *all* of them. They even invent new problems to solve, just to see if they really understand what they have been studying.

Studying with a group of friends is one way to reduce the isolation you experience in learning math. Moreover, it gives you an opportunity to "talk" mathematics. Psychologists believe that we learn most efficiently when we employ all five of our senses. (Mathematicians add another one: the imagination). In fact, expressing new and difficult mathematical ideas orally is a good exercise in learning to think more deeply about what you are doing in math.

Developing Your Own System

The title of this chapter notwithstanding, in some important ways mathematics is not meant to be "read" at all. Its own notation is far better suited to expressing mathematical statements than words are. The instructions in a textbook can be thought of as a kind of scaffolding that is no longer needed once the structure of your understanding is in place. That's why many good math students don't go back to the narrative in their books when they review for an exam—they only review the problems.

Mathematics teachers know this and will often select a textbook not for the clarity of its presentation, but for the quality of its examples and the challenge of its homework problems. They prefer to rely on the text for pacing, as a way of communicating to students how far and how quickly they are supposed to be moving in a particular course. Yet, for those who are unused to that kind of book, it is worth spending some time thinking about how to tackle it, and generating some system for making the best possible, the most efficient, use of the material it provides. That "best use" in all probability will be uniquely your own.

Chapter

3

Problem Solving

Is there one "scientific" way to solve a problem in mathematics? It would be reassuring to think there is a step-by-step procedure that works every time. But there is no one guaranteed "right" way to solve all problems. There may be better ways. One solution may be, as mathematicians put it, more "elegant"; another more useful in the long run because the same technique can be applied to more complex examples. But problem solving is also very individual. What works for one problem solver may not work for another. What works in one type of problem may not work in another. In studying math you probably have come across theories about the 4, 6, or 10 "basic steps" in problem solving, organized in some strict sequence. But almost no one ever *discovers* solutions the first time working so rigidly. After you have arrived at a solution, it is easy to see how you *ought* to have gone about finding it. But few people start out as systematically as they would like.

The aim of this chapter is to help you discover some problem-solving strategies based on the kind of improvising you use in solving puzzles—an approach you may not have thought of applying to mathematics before.

The Puzzle Approach

Suppose you were looking at a colorful 100-piece jigsaw puzzle. Would you expect yourself to be able to pick out 10 pieces at random and put them directly into place? Of course not. If you'd had any experience solving jigsaw puzzles, you would start with a few obvious pieces, probably the edges, and begin to work with them before you had any idea what the puzzle would eventually turn out to be.

You would locate the corners, connect them with the edges, and, as you worked, you would begin to notice a pattern of color or shape emerging. There might be a cluster of blues that could be a sky or a body of water. So, as you were completing your first task, framing the puzzle picture with pieces that had one straight edge, you would already start thinking about collecting the blues. And while considering piece by piece where the blues belonged, you'd begin to notice, perhaps, a yellow sun in the making, or a roof, or a bird.

One of the pleasures in solving puzzles is that, while you need to know where you are going to solve a problem, *you don't have to know how to get there in order to begin.* In fact, the more you work at what appear at first to be trivial tasks (edges and blues), the easier it gets to see the whole. Near the end, the remaining pieces just about propel themselves into place.

Or, take the analogy of a crossword puzzle. You don't stop at square one if you can't think of an answer. Instead, you scan the "down" and the "across" columns for words you are very sure of and begin with them. Only after you have thought of answers to all of the easy clues do you begin to work with the letters you already have in place in search of the elusive ones.

Strategies

You'll notice in solving puzzles that you are using several distinct kinds of problem-solving strategies, but—and this is important—not in any rigid order. You have an initial *strategy* in each case—to find the edges of the jigsaw puzzle, for example. You *search* in a semihaphazard way. You *sort* by some category: color, shape, or meaning. You *guess* and continually refine your guesses as you go along. As you proceed, you are *assessing* your progress. Sometimes you have to shift a piece or a letter when something new appears. So your system involves:

- Initial strategy
- Shifting strategies
- Searching
- Sorting
- Guessing
- Refining the guesses
- Assessing how you are doing
- Continuing to search

These are not steps but methods and strategies you will use in tandem, going from one to the other and back again, experimenting and improvising as you reach for a solution.

Let's go to a particular problem in mathematics and see how the puzzle approach works.

The Bushel Problem

This is an old puzzle that has been around, they say, since the Middle Ages.

One hundred bushels of corn are to be divided among 100 persons. Men get 3 bushels each. Women get 2 bushels each. Children get 1/2 bushel each. How will the bushels be distributed?

Your first observation might be, as mine was, that a key piece of information is missing, namely how many of the 100 people are men, how many are women, and how many are children. I decided to try out one extreme to get going: that there were either no men, no women, or no children in the group. I then tried to see where that would lead me, or, to say it more mathematically, whether that would give me some parameters or constraints (some kind of "edges") to the problem.

Well, if there are no men, then 100 bushels need to be divided among some number of women (at 2 bushels each) and some number of children (at 1/2 bushel each). Fifty women would get 100 bushels,

Figure 8

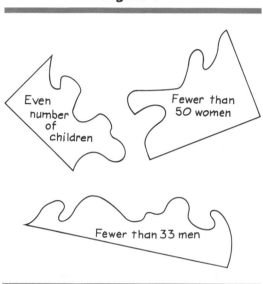

using up the total, so that's clearly not the right strategy. Thirty women use up 60 bushels, leaving 40 bushels to be divided among 70 children. But if 70 children claim 35 bushels, we've only distributed 95. So that's not right either. But, I had already learned something about the constraints (the edges) of the problem. There would have to be an even number of children (to avoid a 1/2 bushel left over), fewer (probably a lot fewer) than 33 men, and fewer than 50 women.

Next, I tried eliminating women. By the same search process, I discovered that 20 men, each getting 3 bushels (60 bushels), plus 80 children, each getting 1/2 bushel (40 bushels), produced one solution. But I had eliminated women, which I preferred not to do. Perhaps by *replacing* numbers of men and children with numbers of women, I might find my way to another solution that did include women.

Guess and Check

What I was involved in at this point was the search strategy. There is no pressure at this stage to do anything more than get familiar with the problem and begin to understand and appreciate its constraints. I guessed at a particular configuration and then checked my guess against the totals, just as you might pick up a piece of a jigsaw puzzle that looked as if it might belong in a particular slot, and then check by trying to fit it into place. If it fit, you would insert it and move on to the next piece. If it didn't fit, you would set it aside and move on. The point is, you don't lose confidence and the will to continue just because your first tries do not work. Each time you make a "mistake" in problem solving, you learn something new about the problem, which makes it easier to guess right the next time.

Guess and check has several advantages, one of which is psychological. While struggling with the problem, guess and check gives you something tangible to do. Guessing requires more invention than knowledge; in fact, it is the most creative part of problem solving. Checking, as you will see, is the more systematic part. The primary disadvantage of guess and check is that it takes a good deal of time. As you develop your own preferred skills and strategies for problem solving, you will become faster, but never apologize for needing or using time.

Let's try to solve the bushel problem by guess and check, using a combination of men, women, and children. You will find an algebraic solution to the problem worked out on page 41. But I think it is interesting and important to see how far you can go without algebra. Remember that while medieval scholars knew some algebraic techniques, they didn't yet have a convenient symbol system with which to work. So, if we are going to be true to that era, we too should solve the problem without algebra.

Replacement Strategy

The incomplete solution that 20 men and 80 children will use up all 100 bushels is one of those "mistakes" that is going to be very useful. At this point it is obvious that we are going to have to reduce the numbers of men and children in order to introduce some women. We can do that by creating a replacement system.

Adding 1 woman means either removing 1 child (and 1/2 bushel) or removing 1 man (and 3 bushels). But since we can't add or remove children except in pairs (we decided that already in order to avoid 1/2 bushels in our total), we will probably have to work in increments of +2 women (+4 bushels) and −2 children (−1 bushel). That particular alteration doesn't solve our problem. But if we try other combinations we will come upon the following that does work:

Replacement Strategy	New Distribution	
+5 women (+10 bushels)	5 women	10 bushels
−2 children (−1 bushels)	78 children	39 bushels
−3 men (−9 bushels)	17 men	51 bushels
	Total 100 people	100 bushels

We have introduced women into our solution and we have assigned 100 bushels to 100 people.

Other Strategies

But suppose we hadn't started with the zero-women option. How much could we do by random guessing and systematically checking our guesses? Let's begin by guessing at a configuration that uses all 100 bushels—say 20 men, 19 women, and 4 children (see Table 1). Then we'll try another that uses all of the people—9 men, 31 women, and 60 children (see Table 2). We're getting closer, with only 19 bushels too many. But the process is going to be very tedious unless we can be more systematic.

Table 1

	Bushels/Person	No. People	No. Bushels
Men	3	20	60
Women	2	19	38
Children	1/2	4	2
Total		43	100

Table 2

	Bushels/Person	No. People	No. Bushels
Men	3	9	27
Women	2	31	62
Children	1/2	60	30
Total		100	119

Very often, and this is a case in point, the checking method leads us to another way of solving the problem if there is one. Note that we didn't start out looking for a formula, which is an abstract way of relating this problem to other, similar problems. Rather, we got involved with the specific problem itself. We got a feel for the problem and developed a systematic checking method (the tables of data). But now it is time to look for a pattern in our results.

The Algebraic Solution

What we are actually doing as we construct these tables of data is multiplying the number of people by the number of assigned bushels per person across each row. We are also adding the number of people in one column and the number of bushels distributed in the other. And, of course, we are trying to get to 100 as the total in each column. We can express our unknowns—the number of men, the number of women, and the number of children—in terms of algebraic symbols for unknowns: x, y, and z. To get 100 people, $x + y + z = 100$ people. To get 100 bushels, $3x + 2y + z/2 = 100$ bushels.

Table 3

	Bushels/Person	No. People	No. Bushels
Men	3	x	$3x$
Women	2	y	$2y$
Children	1/2	z	$z/2$
Total		100	100

Figure 9. Distribution of Bushels

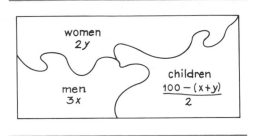

Now we have expressed the problem in two equations with three unknowns, so we next try to substitute to get rid of the z term. Since $z = 100 - (x+y)$, the total number of bushels assigned to children can be expressed as

$$\frac{100 - (x + y)}{2}.$$

Our puzzle is coming a little bit more into shape. By transforming our constraints into unknowns, we can construct another table using just two unknowns (see Table 4). And for the total number of bushels we have the equation

$$3x + 2y + \frac{100 - (x+y)}{2} = 100.$$

At this point we have generated an equation we can use to solve the problem. Plotting the equation on a graph, we can discover the line on the graph that passes through the many solutions (there are more than one) that satisfy all of the requirements of this problem.

Table 4

	Bushels/Person	No. People	No. Bushels
Men	3	x	$3x$
Women	2	y	$2y$
Children	1/2	$100 - (x+y)$	$\dfrac{100 - (x+y)}{2}$

To plot a line on a graph representing the above equation, it is easier to first transform the equation into the form $y = mx + b$. To do that we have to transfer all of the terms other than y in the equation to the right-hand side and leave y alone on the left. To do this manipulation take

$$3x + 2y + \frac{100 - (x+y)}{2} = 100$$

(our previous equation), and multiply both sides by 2:

$$6x + 4y + 100 - (x+y) = 200.$$

Combine x's and y's:

$$5x + 3y = 100$$
$$3y = -5x + 100. \quad \text{Change the sign when you change sides.}$$

Divide both sides by 3:

$$y = \frac{-5}{3}x + \frac{100}{3}.$$

With an equation in the form $y = mx + b$, we can now find the slope (the m term, $\frac{-5}{3}$) and the intercept (b).

The equation, as transformed, can be plotted on a graph (Figure 10). The straight line representing the equation includes *all* of the coordinates that satisfy the equation, but some of these will not be usable solutions to our problem because we are trying to relate to a real-life situation where the solutions—numbers of men, women, and children—will have to be whole numbers. (A solution involving half a child is no solution at all in the real world.) Also, in graphing equations we cannot be certain that our renderings are exact. Still, from this graph, we can read off some probable solutions to the problem. It looks like there are a number of them:

$$x = 20, \quad y = 0$$
$$x = 17, \quad y = 5$$
$$x = 14, \quad y = 10$$

$$x = 11, \quad y = 15$$
$$x = 8, \quad y = 20$$
$$x = 5, \quad y = 25$$
$$x = 2, \quad y = 30$$

We can now go back to our original table and plug in these coordinate pairs (see Table 5). Remember, $z = 100 - (x + y)$ so when we know x and y, we can find z.

Figure 10

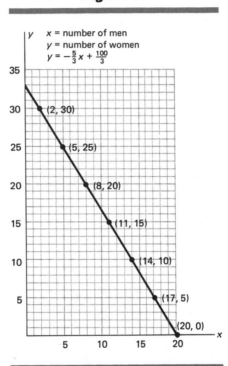

x = number of men
y = number of women
$y = -\frac{5}{3}x + \frac{100}{3}$

(2, 30)
(5, 25)
(8, 20)
(11, 15)
(14, 10)
(17, 5)
(20, 0)

Using a guess-and-check strategy, it took us a long time to find just *one* combination of men, women, and children that satisfied the conditions of the problem. Using an algebraic formula, we've found seven combinations that all work. Such is the power of algebra!

Table 5

x,y	Men	Women	Children 100 − (x + y)	No. People	No. Bushels
20, 0	20	0	80	100	3(20) + 2(0) + 1/2(80) = 100
17, 5	17	5	78	100	3(17) + 2(5) + 1/2(78) = 100
14, 10	14	10	76	100	3(14) + 2(10) + 1/2(76) = 100
11, 15	11	15	74	100	3(11) + 2(15) + 1/2(74) = 100
8, 20	8	20	72	100	3(8) + 2(20) + 1/2(72) = 100
5, 25	5	25	70	100	3(5) + 2(25) + 1/2(70) = 100
2, 30	2	30	68	100	3(2) + 2(30) + 1/2(68) = 100

Nonalgebraic Strategies

But suppose we didn't know or remember this algebraic technique. What else could we have done? To feel comfortable doing problem solving it's important to know there is more than one way to get going.

Let's pick up where we left off with 19 bushels too many and see how we might have continued. Recall our last "guess" (see Table 6). Think about the jigsaw puzzle coming to an end. You have lots of pieces in place, but some of them are still on the table. Think of those as the extra 19 bushels. How can you get rid of 19 bushels within the constraints of the problem? You can't reduce the *total* number of people. If you get rid of 1 man (−3 bushels), you have to add 1 woman (+2 bushels) or 1 child. You cannot do *that*, because you'll end up with a 1/2 bushel in the total. So, instead, let's try exchanging 2 men, 2 women, and/or 2 children at a time.

Table 6

	Bushels/Person	No. People	No. Bushels
Men	3	9	27
Women	2	31	62
Children	60	1/2	30
Total	100		119

Change in No. People		Change in No. Bushels
Reducing	2 men	−6
Adding	2 children	+1
Net change	0 people	−5

If we want to get rid of multiples of 5 bushels, we have found a way: reducing by 2 men and adding 2 children. But +19 isn't a multiple of 5 so how else can we reduce bushels?

Change in No. People		Change in No. Bushels
Reducing	2 women	−4
Adding	2 children	+1
Net change	0 people	−3

We need a combination of −5 and −3 to equal the 19-bushel surplus. We can concoct this combination because twice −5 and three times −3 equals −19, or $2(-5) + 3(-3) = -19$.

If we replace 4 men with 4 children and replace 6 women with 6 children, we have the solution shown in Table 7. Recognizing that in terms of bushel distribution, 5 women = 3 men + 2 children, we can extend our logic to give a number of other solutions (see Table 8).

We've done it. At least six solutions are available to us without a formula, without algebra, just by working from knowns to unknowns without losing our way.

What are the advantages of a step-by-step approach like this one? We already know that this problem-solving technique takes a lot of time and does not give us all the possible solutions to the problem. Still, it is one way we can *get started,* even when we temporarily forget or do not know what else to do. I do not recommend this pre-algebraic method for solving problems with three

Table 7

	Bushels/Person	No. People	No. Bushels
Men	3	5	15
Women	2	25	50
Children	1/2	70	35
Total		100	100

Table 8

	Bushels/Person	No. People	No. Bushels
Men	3	8	24
Women	2	20	40
Children	1/2	72	36
Total		100	100
Men	3	11	33
Women	2	15	30
Children	1/2	74	37
Total		100	100
Men	3	14	42
Women	2	10	20
Children	1/2	76	38
Total		100	100
Men	3	17	51
Women	2	5	10
Children	1/2	78	39
Total		100	100
Men·	3	2	6
Women	2	30	60
Children	1/2	68	34
Total		100	100

variables. Rather, I use it to demonstrate that thinking in mathematics is stimulated by taking a problem apart logically. If we could not recall the formula and techniques used to solve problems of this sort, and didn't have another strategy to try, we might have given up at the start.

The Tire Problem Revisited

We could have applied this strategy to the five-tire problem we talked about earlier. (A car goes 50,000 miles rotating all five tires equally. How far will any one tire have traveled on the road?) We could construct a table to illustrate the sequence of tires (designated a, b, c, d, and e) being rotated and then just add up what is in front of our eyes as follows:

Miles (in thousands)	0–10	10–20	20–30	30–40	40–50
Tires on Car	abcd	bcde	cdea	deab	eabc
Spare	e	a	b	c	d

This layout allows us to see that each of the five tires has been in the trunk only once during the rotation modeled above. That means that each has spent 10,000 miles in the trunk and, subtracting that number of miles from the total journey of 50,000 miles, has been on the road 40,000 miles. Or, without a picture, we could create a unit of "tire miles." If the car goes a total of 50,000 miles, then four tires on the car go a total of 200,000 tire miles. One-fifth of the total 200,000 tire miles would be the share of each tire:

$$\frac{200,000 \text{ tire miles}}{5 \text{ tires}} = 40,000 \text{ miles.}$$

While problems of the tire and bushel variety make for good practice in reasoning, most problems you will encounter in mathematics courses at college are not pure puzzlers like these, but are meant to test your immediate mastery of new material. So, let's turn to an example of a more straightforward math problem, typical of what you are likely to find in your first college course.

Divided-Page Problem Solving

When you're problem solving, using the divided-page approach helps you keep a running record of your ideas and insights. It also helps you keep track of what you are doing and why. The discipline will tend to prevent some common errors (such as putting down wrong units or making careless mistakes in calculation). It also develops your skill in listening to yourself think.

Let's see how one student's divided page gives her a way to solve a classic problem:

A farmer buys 1,000 yards of chain-link fencing. What is the largest rectangular area he can enclose with this amount of fencing?

Figure 11

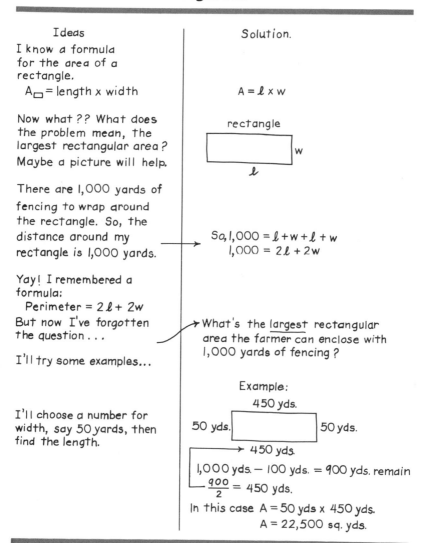

Ideas

I know a formula for the area of a rectangle.

$A_\square$ = length x width

Now what ?? What does the problem mean, the largest rectangular area? Maybe a picture will help.

There are 1,000 yards of fencing to wrap around the rectangle. So, the distance around my rectangle is 1,000 yards.

Yay! I remembered a formula:

Perimeter = 2ℓ + 2w

But now I've forgotten the question . . .

I'll try some examples...

I'll choose a number for width, say 50 yards, then find the length.

Solution.

A = ℓ x w

rectangle

So, 1,000 = ℓ + w + ℓ + w
1,000 = 2ℓ + 2w

What's the largest rectangular area the farmer can enclose with 1,000 yards of fencing?

Example:
450 yds.

50 yds.   50 yds.

450 yds.

1,000 yds. − 100 yds. = 900 yds. remain

$\frac{900}{2}$ = 450 yds.

In this case A = 50 yds x 450 yds.
A = 22,500 sq. yds.

Figure 11 continued

I'll try another example; say width is 100 yards

Another example:

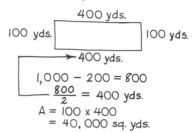

$$1,000 - 200 = 800$$
$$\frac{800}{2} = 400 \text{ yds.}$$
$$A = 100 \times 400$$
$$= 40,000 \text{ sq. yds.}$$

Although I used 1,000 yards of fencing in both examples, I _did_ get different areas from different lengths and widths. When I chose a longer width the area increased. I'll try that again.

More examples:

200 yds. [300 yds.   ] 200 yds.
300 yds.

A = 200 x 300 = 60,000 sq. yds.

The area increased again.

[   ] 300 yds.
200 yds.

Hmm ... The same area. I'd better set up a table.

A = 200 x 300 = 60,000 sq. yds.

Width (yds.)	Length (yds.)	Area (sq. yds.)
50	450	22,000
100	400	40,000
200	300	60,000
300	200	60,000

I see here that a rectangle with width 200 and length 300 is the same as one with width 300 and length 200.

Figure 11 continued

	Width (yds.)	Length (yds.)	Area (sq. yds.)
I'll try more values.	50	450	22,500
	100	400	40,000
	200	300	60,000
	225	275	61,875
This value seems to be the largest. →	250	250	62,500
	275	225	61,875

A rectangle 250 yards x 250 yards is actually a square.

I think the largest rectangular area that can be enclosed by 1,000 yards of fencing is a square area 250 yards x 250 yards.

	Width (yds.)	Length (yds.)	Area (sq. yds.)
I'll try some more values.	50	450	22,500
	100	400	40,000
	200	300	60,000
	225	275	61,875
	249	251	62,499
Now I'm almost certain →	250	250	62,500
that this is the correct	251	249	62,499
answer.	275	225	61,875

Note how relaxed the student is about forgetting first the formula and then the question. She knows that working through the problem and making up examples will help her get unstuck.

Estimation

Many of the real-life problems you will need to be able to think about, if not to solve precisely, are those involving estimation. Often the so-called parameters of the problem (the actual numbers involved) will not be given. Instead, you will have to make some reasonable assumptions in order to get started. But you will still have to have a sense of the problem and some appropriate problem-solving strategies in order to go forward.

Some kinds of estimation challenges are known colloquially as "Fermi problems," after the great twentieth-century nuclear physicist, Enrico Fermi. A typical Fermi problem goes like this: How many piano tuners live and work in the Chicago area? Obviously, unless you cheat and go to the Yellow Pages (although that is certainly an acceptable strategy in solving this real-life problem), you have no way to figure out the answer. But by thinking about the problem for a while, you can at least get started. Estimate how many families live in the Chicago area, and then, from your own experience, what proportion of those families might own their own pianos. Add to this the number of music schools and concert halls that might have more than one piano. (How many more?) Try to find out how long it takes a piano tuner to tune one instrument. Then develop a model of the problem based on your assumptions.

Number of piano tuners in Chicago (n)

So many pianos (x)

So many annual service hours per 1 piano (y)

Total hours to tune all pianos per year (xy) divided by the average number of hours piano tuners work per year (h)

$$n = \frac{xy}{h}$$

It goes without saying that your total will certainly be wrong in that you could not possibly estimate the *exact* number of piano tuners at work in Chicago. But you would be able to get what Fermi called a "back-of-the-envelope calculation." Then you could turn to the Yellow Pages and check your estimate against reality. If you are close, your assumptions were probably realistic.

Business people and planners in just about every field have to do this kind of logical estimation all the time. Here is one example inspired by a recent newspaper article about the decision to build a 15-mile-long light-rail commuter line designed to connect two cities in the state of Oregon. The line will cost $214 million to construct and, according to the report, is going to be able to carry 50,000 riders during a 10-hour day. Those who support mass transportation favored this option. The alternative would have been another four-lane superhighway, costing nearly $500 million to build. Supporters of the highway claim that it would have had a greater commuter capacity than the rail line will have. How could you argue for or against either position?

One way would be to calculate by estimation the number of riders that the four-lane highway might be able to carry in one day. To do this you will have to make some reasonable assumptions—for example, that there are about 6 rush hours in a day when cars would be traveling about 200 feet apart and 4 non–rush hours when cars would be traveling 1,000 feet apart. Also, that the average speed of a car would be 45 miles per hour and that the average passenger load during rush hour would be 1.3 people per car (meaning there are 2 people in every third car), and that during non–rush hour there might be an average of 2 people per car. Four lanes of traffic (2 in each direction) means that you have to multiply the car capacity times 4, or, to put it another way, there are really 60 miles of driving lanes in the 15-mile highway that can be traveled at any one time.

There are a number of ways to model this problem. One is to imagine yourself standing at some point along the highway counting cars as they whiz by, then multiply that number by 6 or 4 hours and multiply that product by 1.3 or 2 passengers depending on the time of day. Or, you might imagine a kind of snapshot of the entire 15 miles of highway at any one time and try to figure out how many cars are on all 4 lanes in that instantaneous picture. Let's try the snapshot model. Using assumptions to get to an estimate, my calculations of the problem are as follows.

Assuming 200 feet between cars during rush-hour traffic, I can calculate a car density of 25 cars per mile and by assuming 1,000 feet per car during non–rush hour, a car density of 5 cars per mile. Multiplying these figures by 4 lanes and 15 miles I come up with the following totals: $25 \times 4 \times 15 = 1,500$ cars during a rush hour, and $5 \times 4 \times 15 = 300$ cars during a non–rush hour. These lines of cars are not static, of course. Some cars are getting on and others are getting off the highway at all times. At what point would the snapshot of cars be entirely replaced by a new set of cars? Calculating the average speed at 45 miles per hour, all of the cars in my snapshot would be off the road in 20 minutes, having traversed the full 15 miles of highway. So, there are 3 different snapshots in any one hour and $1,500 \times 3 = 4,500$ cars in any one rush hour; $300 \times 3 = 900$ cars in any one non–rush hour.

I further assume that there are 6 rush hours in a day and 4 non–rush hours (I do this because the light-rail line that will be built instead of the highway will run 10 hours a day). So, the rush hour car total has to be multiplied by 6: $4,500$ cars $\times 6 = 27,000$ cars. And the non–rush hour total has to be multiplied by 4: $900 \times 4 =$

3,600 cars. That gives a total of 30,600 cars likely to be using the highway in any one normal workday and a total of 42,300 riders (27,000 × 1.3 = 35,100 + 3,600 × 2 = 7,200). Using these assumptions, I get a capacity figure for the highway *smaller* than the 50,000 riders per day that the light-rail will carry, and at more than twice the cost of construction.

Such an estimate is not exact. We have made a number of assumptions, any one of which might be challenged (such as the assumption that there are 200 feet between cars during rush hour). On the other hand, they are reasonable assumptions, and those who would like to see a highway built instead of a rail line will have to demonstrate that they are substantially undervalued. It is probable, in fact, that the proponents of the light-rail line started their analysis with just such an estimate of the likely capacity of the highway and then went about designing a light-rail alternative that would provide more capacity at a lower cost. Estimation is essential in planning. Until a road or a rail line is built no one can really know how many cars or people will use it. Yet, it is important to have some notion of need before beginning construction.

The Fine Art of Problem Solving

What makes for good problem solving? Knowledge of mathematics of course, but also patience, persistence, and experience. It may seem to the beginner that math teachers (or experts) are just pulling next steps out of the air when, in fact, ideas are coming from all of their past experience and close scrutiny of the problem. Keeping track of your thoughts, as with the divided-page technique, pursuing all possibilities, as suggested by the puzzle approach, and lining up your data in the form of tables to help see patterns are just a few of many ways to succeed in problem solving. You will become skilled at these strategies as you gain experience and confidence in this fine art.

But you will get better at it only if you practice and learn how to keep yourself going even as you encounter difficulty. What awaits you if you succeed is the special thrill of discovery: that moment when you can lean back and say "I did it."

Part

II

Thinking
About
Mathematics

Chapter

4

The Wonders
of Pi

Perimeters, Diameters,
and Pi

Every concept in mathematics has two histories. The first is the story of how, during the 10,000 or so years of human history, certain ideas slowly emerged to make sense of the numerical relationships in the world around us. The second is a personal history of how each of us, guided by all of the discoveries that were made before we were born, struggle individually to make sense of that world of numbers for ourselves.

I can still remember how bothered I was the first time a teacher told me about pi. I was in the seventh grade and until then, had trusted mathematics. There was a certainty and a logic in the subject that had given me confidence in it and, by extension, in myself. I could add figures in any direction and they would come out the same. I could check my multiplication with division and my division with multiplication. Doubling always produced even numbers, and if you forgot one item of the multiplication table you could—if you remembered the rest of it—figure out the missing product for yourself.

But pi seemed to have dropped into my familiar world of mathematics from nowhere and in almost mystical garb. It wasn't just the Greek letter for "p" (π) that confounded me. Rather, I wasn't told where pi came from or why it always worked. I was simply instructed to use pi (either the approximate fraction 22/7 or the longer decimal, 3.14159 . . .) whenever I had a circumference or an area of a circle to compute.[1] Like many students, I didn't understand that pi is a constant ratio between the circumference and diameter of any circle. So, I had trouble believing that a single number could apply to circles of any size. Until that moment, "big" and "small" had always seemed significantly different. How could one number come along that would work equally well for circles of vastly different sizes? And why should that number be such a strange one?

Fortunately, I have a patient and generous father who wanted me to understand mathematics the way he does, profoundly and not as a series of formulas to memorize. So one day we cleared a large table, sat down together, and began to explore the problem of pi. First, we looked at figures I was comfortable with—the square, for example—and my father made the connection for me between the "diameter," or any line drawn across a square, and its "perimeter," the measurement around it. We then drew a square and a circle that had the same "diameters."[2] (See Figure 12.)

Once we had written d on the square, he helped me see that with d in place, we could derive a formula for p, the perimeter of the square. Since d was the same length as any one side of the square, I could see that $p = 4d$ would be that formula. Pi, he explained to me, was just like "4" in the formula for the perimeter of a square. Every square has a length that, multiplied by 4, results in the length around it, and every circle has a diameter that, multiplied by π, results in the length around it. So far so good. I began to understand why π worked for circles of any size. After all, 4 times the length worked for squares of any size. That was the beauty

---

1. Pi is a nonrepeating, nonending decimal—an irrational number that will be discussed further on p. 63. The ellipses (three dots), always included in the decimal notation of pi, mean that the decimal goes on beyond the last number shown. If we did not use a symbol like π, there is no way we could write the value of pi exactly.
2. Squares don't really have "diameters" (rather, bisectors) and circles have "circumferences," not perimeters. Because my father and I were trying to establish the similarity between a circle and a square, we used these terms carelessly. In this chapter we shall henceforth use the correct terminology.

Figure 12

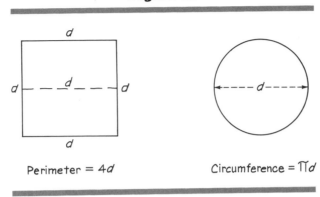

Perimeter = 4*d*   Circumference = Π*d*

of abstraction in mathematics. If perimeter = 4*d*, and circumference = π*d*, then perimeter/*d* = 4 and circumference/*d* = π. This is the constant ratio—4 in the case of squares, π in the case of circles.

But, I still wanted to know why pi was 3.14159 . . . , so we went back to the diagrams. I could see that the circle we had drawn fit inside our square. The circumference of the circle and its area were just a little smaller than those of the square. At each corner, the square extended out beyond the curve of the circle. It should be no surprise, my father pointed out, that pi—this equivalent of 4 for the circle—is a little less than 4. The mystery of π began to recede, but I still didn't understand why it was *always* 3.14159. . . .

Figure 13

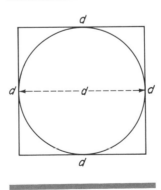

Our next task was to draw a series of circles, all the same size. Then we drew squares, hexagons (six sides), and octagons (eight sides) as well, placing these polygons inside (inscribed) and outside (circumscribed) the circle, as you can see in Figure 14. We were trying to show graphically the relationship between a circle and a straight-sided figure that is easy to measure with a ruler.

Figure 14

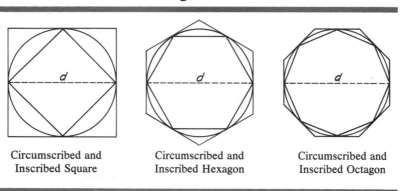

| Circumscribed and Inscribed Square | Circumscribed and Inscribed Hexagon | Circumscribed and Inscribed Octagon |

The Pi Experiment

We used circles with a two-inch diameter. Thus, the inside and outside polygons had two-inch bisectors as well. These are the steps we followed:

1. Draw the polygons inside and outside the circles.
2. Measure the side lengths of each.
3. Calculate the perimeter of each polygon by multiplying the number of sides by the side lengths.
4. Find the ratio between the perimeters of all of the figures and their bisectors.

After drawing these multisided figures inside and outside the three circles, we took a ruler and measured each of their side lengths to get their perimeters. In other words, we treated these multisided figures as if they were circles. Once we had their bisectors and their perimeters, we could calculate the various ratios between their perimeters and bisectors, just as if they were circles.

Our purpose was to determine the ratios between the perimeters and bisectors of all the figures we had drawn and then to compare them to the circumference–diameter ratio of our circles. My father knew something he wanted me to find out for myself.

As we made our various measurements, we began to notice that as the number of sides of a polygon increased, that is, as we went from the square that hardly filled the circle to the octagon that almost filled it entirely, the ratios of perimeter to bisector began to approach the number for pi.

If we had drawn increasingly multisided figures, they would have looked more like circles and our ratio of perimeter to bisector would have been even closer to 3.14159. . . . Had we been able to draw a polygon having an *infinite* number of sides, we would have found the ratio between its perimeter and bisector to be just 3.14159. . . .

My father had demonstrated a "geometric derivation" and through it I came to understand both why pi works for circles of all sizes and that the number 3.14159 . . . is a "limit" that the ratios of other figures tend to approach. As we drew polygons with ever more sides, measuring their perimeters and comparing them to their bisectors, we were heading toward the number 3.14159. . . . We would never get exactly to that number until we drew a perfect circle, but we could get closer and closer to 3.14159 . . . as we drew polygons with more and more sides. The number 3.14159 . . . , then, is a kind of goal, a finish line. And that's precisely what a "limit" is in mathematics.

Table 9 is the result of our work. It gives ratios for polygons of

Table 9. Ratios of Perimeters to Bisectors

	Circumscribed Polygon	Inscribed Polygon
Triangle	5.20	2.60
Square	4.00	2.83
Hexagon	3.46	3.00
Octagon	3.31	3.06
10 sided	3.25	3.09
12 sided	3.22	3.11
13 sided	3.20	3.11
Circle	3.14159 . . .	3.14159 . . .

up to 13 sides. Looking at this table you can see that as the number of sides of the polygons increases, the ratios between perimeters and bisectors of both the inscribed and circumscribed polygons approach pi (3.14159 . . .). You can see, too, that the ratios of the inscribed polygons *increase* toward 3.14159 . . . and the ratios of the circumscribed polygons *decrease* toward 3.14159. . . . Indeed, those ratios all seem to be converging on the limit of pi.

From such data we can create a graph representing this convergence. Figure 15 shows that the two sets of points representing ratios of perimeters to bisectors converge as the number of sides of the polygons increases. Now we can see that the measurements we took were moving toward pi.

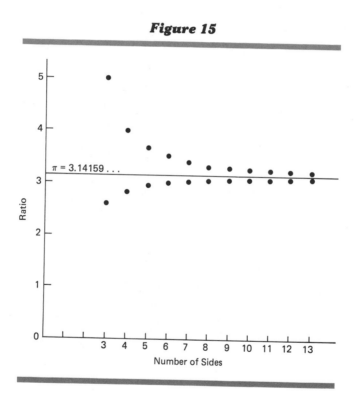

Figure 15

It is possible to use a formula to calculate ratios for many more-sided polygons, which cannot be drawn by hand. Note in Table 10 how the convergence on 3.14159 . . . is even more dramatic.

Table 10. Ratios of Perimeters to Bisectors

Polygon	Circumscribed	Inscribed
64 sided	3.14412	3.14033
128 sided	3.14222	3.14128
256 sided	3.14175	3.14151
512 sided	3.1416321	3.141573
Circle	3.141592 . . .	3.141592 . . .

The Ancients and Pi

Without rulers, using only wet sand as their paper, lengths of rope for measuring, and sticks for marking, ancient peoples were also very interested in finding pi. Primitive as their understanding of mathematics was, there was one observation that could hardly have escaped their notice and that had no exceptions: the greater a circle is across, the longer it is around.

Early man studied this constant ratio, and there are recorded efforts to calculate pi that date from very ancient times. Petr Beckmann, author of *A History of Pi,* believes that the first mathematicians probably tried to calculate pi using a stick and a rope, the way we use a compass, to make a circle in the sand. They laid the rope along the circumference of the circle and, using the diameter of the circle as a unit, counted off the number of diameters along the outstretched rope, one, two, three times. There was still just a little bit left—about 1/6 or 1/7 of a rope length—but it wasn't possible to measure that remaining length too accurately. Hence, we have two calculations of pi deriving from ancient efforts: the Egyptians' 3.1619 and the Babylonians' 3.125.

Rationals and Irrationals

The values given pi by the Egyptians and Babylonians were fairly close to the number used in modern times—3.14159 . . . or, as it is sometimes given in junior high school, 22/7. This fractional form and 3.1416 are both approximations. In fact, pi is not expressible as a fraction since fractions must be *completely expressed* in decimal form, and pi cannot. *Completely expressed* means that when you divide the numerator by the denominator, your result is a decimal that ends in zero or in a block of repeating numbers. Below are two common fractions that can be *completely expressed* in decimal form.

$$\frac{1}{4} = .250 \qquad \frac{1}{8} = .1250$$

Now take the fraction 5/6. If you divide 5 by 6 your calculator will register .8333. You will have as many additional 3s as you have decimal places on your machine. The decimal equivalent of 5/6, .8333, is infinite, like π, but also repeating, unlike π. Do the same with 3/11. The result is also a repeating decimal, this time in a 2-digit pattern (.27272).

Not all repeating patterns are so obvious. Some are four, five, and six digits in length. For example, if you were using a computer rather than a simple calculator (which normally does not have enough decimal places), you could see the long repeating pattern that results from transforming the fraction 22/7 into a decimal.

$$\frac{22}{7} = 3.142857142857142857142857142857142857$$

You would also see that 22/7 is only a crude approximation of pi.

Pi has been calculated to tens of thousands of decimal places with the help of the high speed computation of computers. There is yet no discovery of a repeating pattern of digits (see the first 24 places of pi below) and there never will be because it has been proved in mathematics that pi is an *irrational* number and that's how irrational numbers behave.

$$3.141592653589793238462643 \ldots$$

It just goes on and on, but with no repeating pattern of digits.

Pythagoras and the Discovery of the Irrationals

The ancient Greeks were not just idly speculating about numbers. They were trying to make sense of the numerical relations they observed in the world around them. They were primarily interested in geometry and therefore first came upon irrational num-

Figure 16

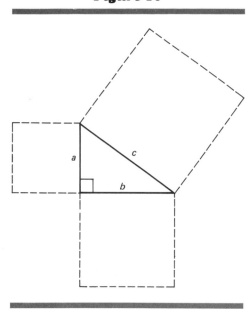

bers when measuring the side lengths of various right triangles. It was Pythagoras (c. 582–500 B.C.) who first stumbled (by geometry) onto his now-famous proof that in every right triangle you can construct a square on each of the three sides and the sum of the *areas* of the squares on either side of the right angle will equal the area of the square constructed on the hypotenuse (Figure 16). You will recall this theorem as: $a^2 + b^2 = c^2$, where a and b are the sides of the right triangle and c is the hypotenuse (Figure 17).

Figure 17

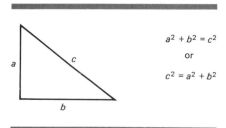

$$a^2 + b^2 = c^2$$

or

$$c^2 = a^2 + b^2$$

This was all very well in geometry. But when numbers entered into the measurement of actual triangles, the arithmetic—as then understood—did not always fit. Right triangles measuring 3, 4, 5 posed no problem because $3^2 + 4^2$ equals 5^2 ($9 + 16 = 25$) (Figure 18). Right triangles measuring 5, 12, 13 nicely totaled $5^2 + 12^2$

Figure 18

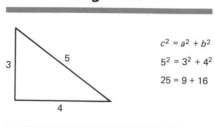

$$c^2 = a^2 + b^2$$
$$5^2 = 3^2 + 4^2$$
$$25 = 9 + 16$$

equals 13^2 ($25 + 144 = 169$) (Figure 19). These are the easy ones and today they are known as Pythagorean triples in honor of Pythagoras. But other just as common right triangles do not produce such neat arithmetic solutions. The triangle with side lengths 1 and 1, for example, has a hypotenuse of $\sqrt{2}$. The triangle with side lengths 9 and 10 has a hypotenuse of $\sqrt{181}$ (Figure 20).

Now the Greeks knew from their geometric proof that the hypotenuse squared had to be the sum of the squares of both side lengths which meant there had to be numbers equivalent to $\sqrt{2}$ and $\sqrt{181}$. But they did not have such numbers in their number system. (We do: Today we calculate $\sqrt{2}$ as 1.414 . . . and $\sqrt{181}$ as 13.453 . . . .) So they called these strange creatures the *irrationals,* meaning numbers that cannot be *completely expressed as ratios,* neither decimals nor fractions.

Pythagoras was both a mathematician and a mystic. He founded a quasi-religious sect whose members were so thoroughly impressed

Figure 19

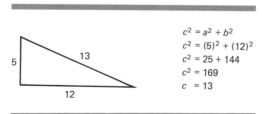

$$c^2 = a^2 + b^2$$
$$c^2 = (5)^2 + (12)^2$$
$$c^2 = 25 + 144$$
$$c^2 = 169$$
$$c = 13$$

Figure 20

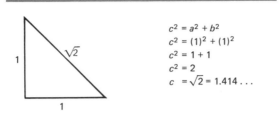

$$c^2 = a^2 + b^2$$
$$c^2 = (1)^2 + (1)^2$$
$$c^2 = 1 + 1$$
$$c^2 = 2$$
$$c = \sqrt{2} = 1.414\ldots$$

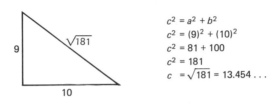

$$c^2 = a^2 + b^2$$
$$c^2 = (9)^2 + (10)^2$$
$$c^2 = 81 + 100$$
$$c^2 = 181$$
$$c = \sqrt{181} = 13.454\ldots$$

with the regularity of numbers that they thought the Creator must have been a mathematician. A story is told that after discovering the frequency of irrational numbers in geometry, Pythagoras went a little crazy and called off his math-based religion. One of his followers is said to have killed himself over irrational numbers. (In other versions of the story, that person was murdered for having discovered them.) Some people apparently didn't want to live in a world where numbers and lengths do not exactly fit.

What was so upsetting logically and psychologically to early Greek mathematicians was the fact that while they could construct right triangles of real lengths and connect these with real hypotenuses, very few right triangles had hypotenuses of rational lengths. Since there are significantly more irrational than rational numbers in right-triangle calculations, you may begin to wonder, as the Greeks did, whether there are more irrational than rational numbers in the universe. There are and it can be proved.

Infinities

There is no limit to how many numbers you can imagine. If you doubt this, try to think up the "last" or "largest" number of all.

You can't, as you'll see more clearly in Chapter 5. Therefore, the total number of rational numbers (those that can be expressed as fractions or repeating decimals) must be infinite. And, by the same logic, the total number of irrational numbers must be infinite, too. Infinity, you would think, is indivisible. So, how could there be two infinities, one even larger than the other? Mathematicians are convinced that there is more than one level of infinity and that the infinity made up of irrational numbers, designated by the Hebrew letter aleph, $\aleph$, is larger than the infinity made up of rational numbers.

This speculation about kinds and sizes of infinities has had important applications in recent mathematical theory and has led to one of the most fruitful lines of mathematical thinking and research in the area of *set theory*.

Functions and Limits

The kind of discovery my father and I were pursuing as we increased the number of sides of polygons and measured their perimeters and bisectors involved two key aspects of modern scientific research: change and constancy. We were conducting a kind of experiment by altering the number of sides of our polygons and then observing the resulting change in the lengths of the perimeters and in the ratios between the perimeters and bisectors. In more general terms, we were altering the independent variable (the number of sides) and measuring the effect this had on the dependent variable (the resulting ratio).

In college mathematics, the value of 3.14159 . . . , toward which our ratios were converging, is called a *limit*. We approach this limit by means of closer and closer approximations until the difference between our measured ratio and the limit is as small as we wish it to be.

The Limit of a Function

An expression like $1/x$ is a "function of x" in mathematics, a dependency relationship. As x changes, the value of $1/x$ changes correspondingly, as you can readily see by substituting numbers for x.

$$\text{If } x = 2, \quad \text{then } \frac{1}{x} = \frac{1}{2}.$$

$$\text{If } x = 12, \quad \text{then } \frac{1}{x} = \frac{1}{12}.$$

This is true even if x is a fraction.

$$\text{If } x = \frac{1}{3}, \quad \text{then } \frac{1}{x} = \frac{1}{\frac{1}{3}} = 3.$$

We can already see that as x increases, $1/x$ grows smaller, but what is the limit of this function? How small could $1/x$ ever get?

$$\text{If } x = 16, \quad \text{then } \frac{1}{x} = \frac{1}{16}.$$

$$\text{If } x = 100, \quad \text{then } \frac{1}{x} = \frac{1}{100}.$$

$$\text{If } x = 1{,}000{,}000, \quad \text{then } \frac{1}{x} = \frac{1}{1{,}000{,}000},$$

growing still smaller, approaching but never quite reaching zero. Mathematicians describe this relationship as follows: As x tends to infinity, $1/x$ approaches zero. The mathematical form of this statement is written

$$\lim_{x \to \infty} \frac{1}{x} = 0.$$

The same pattern holds in the opposite direction. When x grows smaller, $1/x$ approaches infinity.

$$\text{If } x = 2, \quad \text{then } \frac{1}{x} = \frac{1}{2}.$$

$$\text{If } x = \frac{1}{2}, \quad \text{then } \frac{1}{x} = 2.$$

$$\text{If } x = \frac{1}{100}, \quad \text{then } \frac{1}{x} = 100, \text{ and so on.}$$

As x becomes smaller, $1/x$ becomes larger. Or, to say it in mathematical terms, as x tends to zero, the limit of $1/x$ is infinity, which is written

$$\lim_{x \to 0} \frac{1}{x} = \infty.$$

The Smooth Curve of Change

It is common in all scientific experiments to manipulate the independent variable(s) as we did in our pi experiment and to observe the corresponding changes in the dependent variables. In fact, change is so commonly studied in science that a Greek letter has been designated to stand for the difference, or increment, between *what is now* and *what was* before the conditions were altered. That Greek letter is delta and is written Δ.

For example, if the present time is t seconds (some number of seconds from the time an experiment began), then a moment later will be expressed as

$$t + \Delta t \text{ seconds.}$$

While there are examples in nature of so-called *incremental* or *discontinuous change* (mostly at the atomic level), the kinds of change we experience in the macroscopic world tend to occur in a continuous fashion, that is, they are smooth and without interruption. To heat a room from 32°F to 68°F in no matter how short a time, for example, the temperature of the room will pass through every degree and every fraction of a degree between those two extremes. We may not be able to measure every degree or fraction of a degree of change in temperature because our instrumentation is inadequate. But that doesn't mean change in temperature is not going on continuously. So we have to have a way to express *continuous change* mathematically if we are to understand it.

Figure 21 shows how the change in the temperature of a room from 32°F to 68°F over a period of an hour might be described by a graph.

We could just as well describe that temperature change if, in

Figure 21

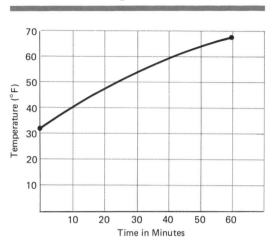

the middle of its heating up, someone were to come in to the room and open a window. The decrease in temperature would be just as continuous as the increase in temperature. And then if someone else came in and closed the window, the room would start heating up again continuously. Figure 22 shows what the temperature change would look like.

Practically, of course, change cannot always be measured continuously because standard instruments can only measure at certain intervals, however small. Where change is continuous, this must be reflected in our equations. A student who only knows how to use whole numbers and fractions will be unable to handle problems dealing with continuous change. This is why an understanding of functions, with their capacity for expressing continuous change, is so important.

The Mathematics of Acceleration

Conditions other than temperature, such as time and velocity, also change in a continuous fashion. It may seem to you when you are driving a car or flying in an airplane that the vehicle moves in steps from the starting speed to the next higher speed. But, in fact,

Figure 22

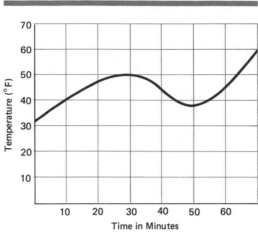

a car accelerating will move through every velocity (and every fraction of a velocity) between the two speeds on its way from one to the other.

One way to get a feel for continuous change is to recall what it is like to be in an airplane during takeoff. Takeoff speed is between 190 and 220 miles per hour. That means the pilot won't point the nose up until that ground speed is achieved. It takes a substantial thrust (force) for an aircraft to accelerate from a standstill velocity of 0 miles per hour to 200 miles per hour; and to do so in less than 40 seconds and within a distance of about 5,000 feet (1 mile) is truly remarkable.

If you had a stopwatch that registered fractions of a second and could observe the exact distance covered on the ground during takeoff, the kind of data you would collect would be like that in Table 11.

The graph of the distance covered by the airplane over time in seconds would look like Figure 23. The plot on the graph representing distance over time is curved and increasingly steep. So, we can conclude that the changing *slope* and the rate at which the airplane is moving forward (that is, its speed) are related. The average speed during the first 1,000 feet is a mere 66 feet/second or 45 miles per hour. But during the third 1,000 feet, the aircraft is

Table 11

Position of Airplane (in feet)	Total Elapsed Time (in seconds)	Time Interval (in seconds)	Average Speed During Interval (in feet/second)
0	00.0		
		15.2	66
1,000	15.2		
		6.3	159
2,000	21.5		
		4.8	208
3,000	26.3		
		4.1	244
4,000	30.4		
		3.6	278
5,000	34.0		

moving at an average speed of 208 feet/second or 142 miles per hour. The *change* in speed is taking place so fast that the first 1,000 feet of travel take up almost one half the total travel time (15.2 seconds); the last 1,000 feet only 3.6 seconds.

Figure 23

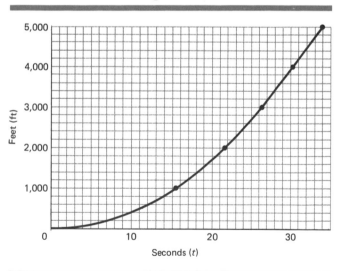

As the aircraft moves down the runway at greater and greater speeds, it covers the same interval of distance in fewer and fewer seconds. In miles per hour, the average speed would be changing as seen in Table 12.

Table 12

Position (in feet)	Average Speed During Time Interval (in mph)
0–1,000	45
1,001–2,000	108
2,001–3,000	142
3,001–4,000	166
4,001–5,000	190

An aircraft's *average speed* while taking off, then, is not very interesting because it is passing through an infinite number of *different speeds* during a very short period of time. What's more interesting and harder by far to calculate is the aircraft's *instantaneous speed*, that is, its speed during takeoff at any one instant in time.

Let's say you're a physicist and you want to calculate the "instantaneous speed" of the airplane at exactly 28 seconds after

Table 13

Interval (in seconds)	Change in Seconds (delta time) Δt	Change in Feet (delta distance) Δd	Speed (in feet/second) ft/sec
25–28	3	651.7	217.2
26–28	2	442.7	221.4
27–28	1	225.4	225.4
27.5–28	.5	113.7	227.4
27.9–28	.1	22.91	229.13
27.99–28	.01	2.2950	229.50
27.999–28	.001	0.22953	229.53
27.9999–28	.001	0.02295	229.54

it starts. Your technique will be to find an average speed over some distance and then narrow the interval. You might begin by calculating the speed in the 3-second interval between 25 seconds and 28 seconds after the start. Then you might shorten this to a .5-second interval and calculate the speed between 27.5 and 28.0 seconds. You can shorten the interval still more to a .1-second interval, even to a .0001-second interval. What you arrive at with these calculations is a *limiting value* that gives you, eventually, as close an approximation as you want of the aircraft's *instantaneous speed* at exactly 28 seconds after takeoff. The calculations are shown in Table 13. The *instantaneous speed* at 28 seconds is 229.54 ft/sec, or 156.50 mph if you had figured this out in miles per hour.[3]

You could have reached the same result by choosing any interval and narrowing it: calculating time intervals with 28 seconds in the middle, such as the speed between 26 and 30 seconds, then the speed between 27.5 and 28.5 seconds, and so on. As you can see, as the length of the time intervals decreases, the speed approaches a limiting value in much the same way that our perimeter–bisector ratios approach pi as the number of sides of the polygons increase. In physics, the change in position is expressed as Δx. The change in time is written Δt. The average speed is the change in position over the change in time, or

$$\frac{\Delta x}{\Delta t}.$$

In mathematical shorthand, then, the expression for instantaneous velocity is written

$$\lim_{\Delta t \to 0} \frac{\Delta x}{\Delta t}.$$

In words, this would be expressed as the limit of the average speed as the duration in time approaches zero.

In college-level courses in mathematics, statistics, and the natural sciences you will learn a powerful technique for finding the rate

---

3. Here's where the conversion tables at the back of many mathematics and science texts come in handy. To convert from feet per second to miles per hour, look up the appropriate conversion table and you will find: 1 mph = 1.467 ft/sec. The rest is division on your calculator.

at which change is taking place. Once you master this technique, which is based on the concept of the limit, you will have a skill you can use in many other areas. In economics, for example, the *average* cost of producing an item may not be nearly as interesting to a manufacturer, who wants to maximize profit, as the cost of that item *at the margin*. The cost of the next item that is produced could be a lot less than the average cost since the factory is in high gear. The technique for calculating cost *at the margin* is identical to that for calculating instantaneous velocity because, as you will see when you take calculus, both involve *measuring the slope of a curve at a particular point on that curve.* Chapter 9 includes an explanation of how this applies to real-life situations.

$$\pi r^2$$

Pi is not only used for finding circumferences; it is also part of the formula discovered by the ancient Greeks for finding the area of a circle. They knew how to calculate the areas of rectangles, triangles, and other polygons, so they decided to proceed from knowns to unknowns in their quest for a way to calculate the areas of circles and other figures not bounded by straight lines. One idea was to subdivide a circle into many triangles, or into many rectangles. Since they knew how to find the area of a triangle or a rectangle, they could fill a circle nearly full with either of these measurable

Figure 24

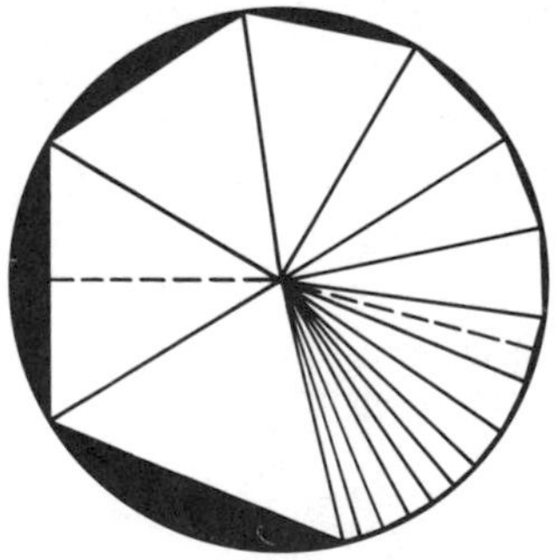

figures, reducing the fraction of the leftover segments, and thereby finding the area of a circle.

Of course, the triangles, even the smallest ones, would never conform *exactly* to the pie-shaped segments in the circle. But the more triangles they drew, the smaller each became and the more nearly it fit into the circle. The remaining spaces, as you can see from the darkened portions of the circle in Figures 24 and 25, become smaller as the triangles become increasingly narrow. They

Figure 25

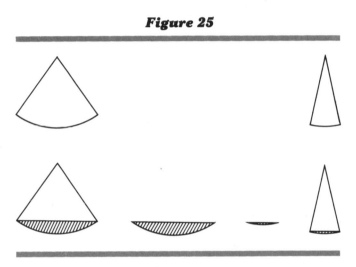

also noticed that as the triangles got smaller, the height of each one corresponded more and more closely to the radius of the circle (Figure 26). Therefore, they figured that if they could draw and then measure the tiniest of triangles, the total measurement of the bases those triangles would be pretty close to the circumference of the circle and the height of each tiny triangle would closely approximate

Figure 26

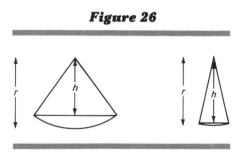

the radius of the circle. Hence they could apply the formula for the area of a triangle to find the area of a circle (see Figure 27).

The problem with this logic was that no matter how small the triangles became, they would never perfectly duplicate the rounded pie-shaped segments they were supposed to represent. So, the

Figure 27

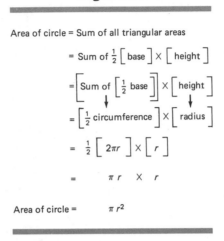

Area of circle = Sum of all triangular areas

$$= \text{Sum of } \tfrac{1}{2} \left[\text{ base } \right] \times \left[\text{ height } \right]$$

$$= \left[\text{Sum of } \left[\tfrac{1}{2} \text{ base } \right] \right] \times \left[\text{ height } \right]$$

$$= \left[\tfrac{1}{2} \text{ circumference } \right] \times \left[\text{ radius } \right]$$

$$= \tfrac{1}{2} \left[\; 2\pi r \; \right] \times \left[\; r \; \right]$$

$$= \qquad \pi \, r \quad \times \quad r$$

Area of circle = $\qquad \pi \, r^2$

Greeks considered that if it were possible (though they knew it wasn't in the real world) to draw an *infinite* number of triangles within a circle, then the space left over in each segment would become infinitely small or very nearly zero. Remember what you learned about expressing limits. As the number of triangles goes to infinity, the difference in area between the pie segment and each tiny triangle approaches zero. This means that the limit of the sum of the areas of all the tiny triangles is equal to the area of the circle as the number of triangles, N, approaches infinity. Or, in mathematical shorthand:

$$\lim_{N \to \infty} (\text{sum of triangle areas}) = \text{area of circle.}$$

Later, mathematicians found that working with rectangles was even more useful in approximating areas within circles and areas under different shaped curves. Think about an architect designing a fence with a curved shape like Figure 28. Fence material doesn't

Figure 28   *Figure 29*

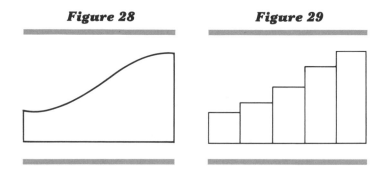

come in curved surfaces, so he will need to buy rectangular slats of varying heights to create a shape like Figure 29. It doesn't look exactly like the curved design but it is beginning to approximate it. If he were to add slats of increasingly narrower widths, the fence would look more and more curved, like Figure 30.

The ancient Greek Archimedes (c. 287–212 B.C.) already understood and applied this technique. In the seventeenth century, that technique evolved—in the hands of Isaac Newton and Gottfried Leibnitz—into integral calculus. Integration, as you will learn in first-year calculus, is a way of "summing" the tiniest rectangular segments of area under a curve to calculate the total area. The mathematical symbol is $\int$.

So, to get the total area of our slatted fence (to calculate the amount of building material needed to construct it, or the gallons of paint needed to cover it), we would take the area of each slat individually, width being represented as Δx, height as y, (area = $y\Delta x$) and then imagine the slats to be decreasing in width, and hence increasing in number. At some point we would contemplate a *limit*

Figure 30

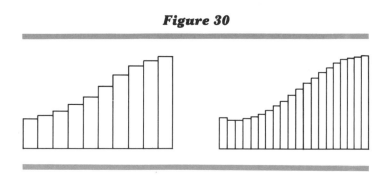

where the slats are thin as a line and numerous as infinity and express that limit as

$$\lim_{\Delta x \to 0} \; (\text{sum of } y\Delta x) = \text{area}.$$

This would be expressed in words as the limit where Δx—the width of each slat—approaches zero and the number of slats approaches infinity. This is how the area of the fence under the curve is defined mathematically.

Exploring Math Through Logic

I think about mathematics as a partially known territory mapped with logic—a territory that can be explored in a number of different ways. One way is to approach the subject historically and to study mathematical ideas in the order in which they were developed. Another is to learn mathematical concepts in order of their increasing difficulty. Not surprisingly, the latter method is the way math is taught practically all over the world. You would not normally find material on pi and integration in the same lesson because one concept is considered far more difficult than the other.

In this chapter, we did something different. We started with a seventh grader's reluctance to accept the notion of pi, and went from there to look a little more closely at geometry (the evolution of the circle from multisided polygons); at set theory (rational versus irrational numbers, different infinities); at some of the fundamental ideas of differential calculus (finding slopes); and at integral calculus (finding the area under a curve) as well.

Students who like mathematics find they don't have to memorize facts. They can figure things out as they go along. One idea in mathematics seems to nest comfortably inside another, as this chapter demonstrates. So, my theory is that if you start somewhere, just about anywhere, you can (with help) explore the system as a whole and at your own pace.

What keeps you going is your curiosity. Arithmetic, says mathematician Peter Hilton, involves going from a question to an answer. True mathematics, he means, takes you from answers to questions.

If the math lesson you are struggling with raises more questions than it answers, don't berate yourself for being "dumb" or slow. Give yourself credit for having the imagination and the curiosity to be pressing the limits of your understanding. Be assertive. Take your questions seriously and persuade your instructor to take them seriously, too. Your responsibility is to phrase your questions as precisely as you can. Your instructor's responsibility is to find a way to help you answer them.

Chapter

5

Taming Numbers

The world of mathematics is made up of more than numbers; it includes functions, variables, geometric shapes, and notation for complex operations. Still, numbers, and the quantities they represent, are an important component of mathematics and in this chapter we shall look more closely at how numbers behave.

Large and Small Numbers

How large (and small) can numbers be? And how can they be handled efficiently in higher mathematics? Much philosophical speculation among the ancient Greek mathematicians had to do with finding the very largest, or, as they put it, the "last" possible number. You have probably heard children arguing that a trillion, trillion, trillion is the largest number, only to be topped by some very canny child who simply adds one or multiplies the last large number by two. This was precisely the puzzle that intrigued the Greeks. If every apparently last or largest number can be added on to or increased by multiplication, how will we ever get to the very largest, or the very last, number of all?

Prime Numbers

It did not take the Greeks too long to decide that there is no last or largest number. Soon they stopped looking for it. But for a while, before Euclid (c. 300 B.C.), they continued to seek something else: the last or largest "prime number." A prime number is a number that is not divisible by any number but itself (and by the number 1, which, of course, can be divided into every number). If a very large number could always be doubled or multiplied by another number, perhaps there was a last number that was not the result of prior multiplication.

Numbers like 7, 11, 263, and 10,006,721 are prime numbers. They are not divisible by any number other than themselves and by 1. But, as the table of primes below indicates, there are fewer prime numbers as one counts higher. The reason for this is pretty clear: the larger the number, the more likely it is that it has divisors other than 1. (Such numbers are called composite numbers.)

Table 14. Prime Numbers

0–100	101–200	201–300	301–400
1,2,3	101,103,107	211,223,227	307,311,313
5,7,11	109,113,127	229,233,239	317,331,347
13,17,19	131,149,151	241,251,257	349,353,359
23,29,31	163,167,173	263,269,271	367,373,379
41,43,47	179,181,191	277,281,283	383,389,397
53,59,61	193,197,199	293	
67,71,73			
79,83,89			
97			

Before Euclid proved that there is no last prime, it seemed logical that there might be, if one counted high enough, a last prime number after which all other large numbers would be composite numbers. Today, everyone knows that just as there is no largest number, so there is no last prime. Still, the search for larger and larger primes continues. That search is not only challenging, but potentially useful since large prime numbers can provide the bases of international security codes.

One recent attempt to locate the largest prime ever was undertaken by two enthusiastic 15-year-old high school students in Hayward, California, in 1975. By then, people had been looking for very large primes for thousands of years. With the help of the computer, some very large numbers had been generated, numbers having thousands of digits not divisible by any number other than themselves or 1. But Laura Nickel and Curt Noll wanted to see if they could go still higher and find a yet larger prime. Three years later, they succeeded in proving that a number having 6,533 digits is a prime.

$2^{21,701} - 1$ Two raised to the 21,701st power, less one.

The technique in searching for new primes is to take a number you have reason to believe might be a prime and then test it extensively to make certain that it is not divisible by any numbers but itself and 1. The solution for Nickel and Noll represented a complicated computer-programming challenge that involved multiplying and subtracting numbers with thousands of digits. Their feat, reported in the January 1979 issue of *Scientific American,* required writing five different versions of their computer program before they began testing numbers. After some 350 hours of their "run," they succeeded in identifying and proving their prime.

Looking for large primes is not a task for the faint of heart. For the majority of us ordinary human beings, it is far more interesting to examine more generally how quantities grow.

How Quantities Grow

Large and small numbers are directly related. A very large number placed in the denominator of a fraction whose numerator is 1 produces a very small number.

221,701 is a very large number.

$\dfrac{1}{221,701}$ is a very small number.

To find out what makes quantities grow, we are going to start by looking at some of the most common kinds of quantitative growth: doubling numbers, expressed in algebraic notation as $2x$; squaring numbers, expressed as x^2; cubing numbers, expressed as x^3; and, finally, *exponential growth,* where the exponent itself in-

Table 15. The Values of $2x$, x^2, x^3, and 2^x as x Increases

x	$2x$	x^2	x^3	2^x
1	2	1	1	2
2	4	4	8	4
3	6	9	27	8
4	8	16	64	16
5	10	25	125	32
6	12	36	216	64
7	14	49	343	128
8	16	64	512	256
9	18	81	729	512
10	20	100	1,000	1,024
11	22	121	1,331	2,048
12	24	144	1,728	4,096

Figure 31

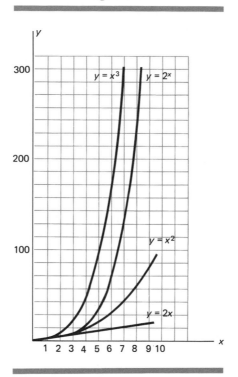

creases, written as 2^x (the expression could be any integer to the xth power). Exponents like 2, 3, and x in the examples given above are written above and are read as x-squared, x-cubed, and 2 raised to the x-th power or 2 to the x-th. There are also *subscripts* in mathematical notation, numbers and letters that are written *under* the line, as in x_1 and x_2, which are read as x sub 1, x sub 2. A mathematician or scientist will write x_1, x_2, x_3, instead of x, y, z, for reasons of economy or clarity. Do not confuse subscripts and exponents. Table 15 and Figures 31 and 32 show how quantities grow in each of these four modes.

Figure 31 shows how these growing patterns are graphed. Only $y = 2x$ appears as a straight line on the graph in Figure 31. All other sketches are curved, because they involve exponents greater than 1. While $y = x^3$ and $y = 2^x$ appear to grow similarly—up to 300 units on this graph—the far greater growth rate of 2^x is apparent on the graph in Figure 32, which is extended to 4,000 units.

Figure 32

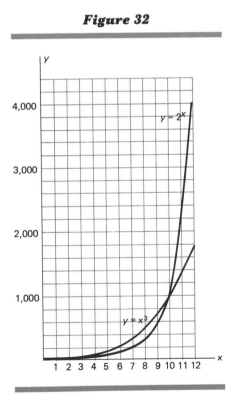

Exponential Growth

As you can see in Figure 32, x^3 takes off at a rapid rate of growth in the lower values of x, but the constant doubling effect of 2^x eventually delivers the most rapid rate of increase. While x^2 and x^3 have exponents, of the four cases developed here only 2^x exhibits what is called *exponential growth*.

Factorials

In 1979, a few months after my book *Overcoming Math Anxiety* was published, Charles Schulz, creator of the Peanuts cartoon, offered his view of math anxiety. The answer to the problem posed

© 1979 United Feature Syndicate, Inc.

in the cartoon is 362,880. It is hard to believe at first but that is how many different ways there are of arranging 9 books on a shelf, so long as each arrangement is counted separately. It helps to think about it in terms of *positions*: For the first position, there are 9 books to choose from, and for each of these 9 choices for the first position, there are 8 choices for the second. That means there are 72 ways just to fill the first 2 positions on the shelf. And for *each* of these 72 choices, there are 7 ways to fill the third position, and so on. The solution to the problem, therefore, is a succession of multiplications.

$$9 \times 8 \times 7 \times 6 \times 5 \times 4 \times 3 \times 2 \times 1 = 362,880$$

To avoid writing out a long string of figures, a problem like this one can be expressed as

$$9!$$

This is read as "nine factorial" and means that you successively multiply every integer between 9 and 1. Contrast 3! with 9! above:

$$3! = 3 \times 2 \times 1 = 6.$$

Factorials grow spectacularly when you consider that the difference between the integers 3 and 9 is only 6 but the difference between their factorials is 362,874.

You may wonder how factorials are used to solve practical problems. Let's consider airline scheduling. An airplane flying to some eventual destination must make stops in 4 cities: Anytown, Boomtown, Cowtown, and Downtown. How many different routes can the pilot take? If you letter the towns A, B, C, and D, you can begin to count routes (see Figure 33).

Figure 33

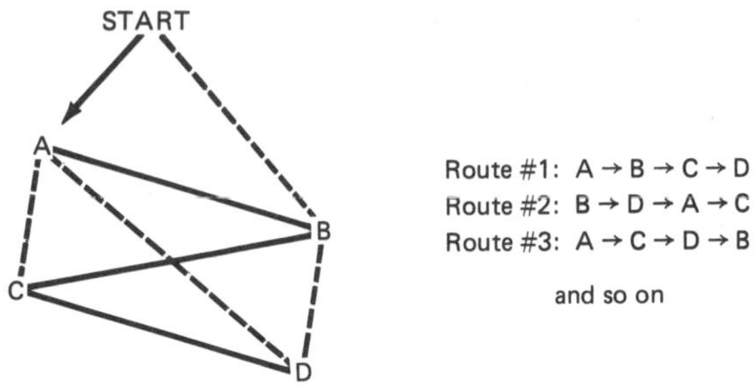

Route #1: A → B → C → D
Route #2: B → D → A → C
Route #3: A → C → D → B

and so on

A more systematic approach is to make a tree diagram, so called because of its resemblance to the branches of a tree. At the start, the pilot has 4 choices of cities for the first stop. At that stop (see line 1 in Figure 34), there are 3 next-choice destinations for each of the 4 choices that might have been made at the beginning. Four choices times 3 choices totals 12 possibilities (see line 2), just for routing through the first 2 cities.

At the next choice point (see line 2 to line 3), the pilot has a selection of 2 different cities for *each* of the 12 routes. Now, the choices can be expressed numerically as: 4 (line 1) × 3 (line 2) × 2 (line 3) through the first 3 cities, or 24 different routes. For the

Figure 34

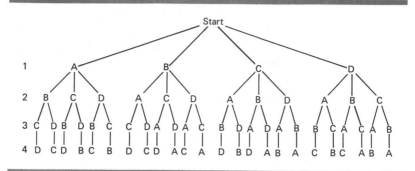

last stop, there is 1 remaining choice possible for *each* of the 24 routes.

This is another example of factorial growth. Since, for the first stop, there are 4 different choices, 3 for the second, 2 for the third, and 1 for the fourth; the solution to the question of how many routes a pilot can take through 4 different cities is the product of $4 \times 3 \times 2 \times 1$, which is 24. The problem could have been expressed as 4! and the meaning would have been just as clear to people who understand mathematical notation.

Applying Exponentials

There are many uses of these growth operations and they show up all the time in the real world. For example, they are employed to estimate population increase over a given period of time.

How Fast Is the Population Growing?

The population of the world was 2.51 billion in 1950, 4.6 billion in 1982, and reached 5 billion in 1986. In the years since 1950 the world's population nearly doubled. Barring a war or a plague, the population of the planet could be 10 billion by the year 2020 if the current growth rate continues.

The only information needed to calculate mathematically a population growth rate per year are two population counts, such as 2.51 billion in 1950 and 4.6 billion in 1982, and the number of years (32) that elapsed in between. The mathematical task is to take the thirty-second root (because 32 years have passed between 1950 and 1982) of the ratio of 4.6 and 2.51 billion. If you have a scientific calculator you will be able to perform the following operation to find the growth rate.

$$\text{Ratio of } \frac{4.6}{2.51} \frac{\text{(1982 population)}}{\text{(1950 population)}} = 1.83$$

Enter 1.83

Key in 1/32 in decimals (years between 1950 and 1982) = 0.03125

Press y^x

Result: 1.019 (called the *multiplier*), which means a *growth rate* of .019 or nearly 2 percent per year.

Check this result with your calculator. Multiply 2.51 (billion) by 1.019 thirty-two times. You should get 4.6 (billion), the population in 1982. Now, to estimate the world's population in the year 2020, you would multiply 2.51 (billion) by 1.019 seventy times, since there are 70 years between 1950 and 2020. This produces a result of approximately 10.2 (billion) people, the probable population of this planet in 2020, if the growth rate remains about 2 percent per year.

Population experts don't like to do 32 or 70 multiplications in sequence even on their calculators. To estimate populations, given a known growth rate, they use a tried-and-true formula involving the current population multiplied by the irrational number e raised to an exponent made up of a growth rate times the elapsed time. The formula applied to the question of the size of the world's population in 2020 is:

$$2.51 \text{ (billion) } e^{kt},$$

where k = an annual growth rate in decimals and t = 70. The same formula could be used to find the world's population in *any* future year by changing the value of t.

Math and Music

In the early part of the seventeenth century, a keyboard instrument called the clavier, a forerunner of the modern piano, was coming into greater use in the musical circles of Europe. This instrument had 12 keys per octave, each key having its own discrete pitch, which made for some difficulty in blending the tones of the clavier with those of the string instruments it accompanied. The string instrumentalist slides the fingers along a fingerboard, creating many subtle variations of pitch. The problem was how to tune the clavier to the strings; how to create a standard scale of evenly distributed pitch for the clavier.

It turns out that tuning a standard 12-key octave on any keyboard instrument is a problem in mathematics, though the composers and tuners of the seventeenth century were not themselves mathematicians. Sound frequency, or vibrations per second, doubles as you go up an octave. For example, the sound frequency of the modern A above middle C is 440 vibrations per second, that of the next higher A, 880. The objective in tuning an instrument with 12 keys to an octave is to have equal intervals (equal frequency ratios) between all 12 keys. In mathematics that desired interval can be calculated. It is the twelfth root of the ratio between these two A notes: $880/440 = 2$. So it is the twelfth root of 2, written $\sqrt[12]{2}$.

Using a scientific calculator you can find that the twelfth root of 2 is 1.0595. That means the interval between the sound frequencies of A and A#, for example, will be 1.0595; and the interval between A# and B, the same, on up the scale.

In Western music, the standard scale described above was established about the time of Johann Sebastian Bach, and the composer's famous set of preludes and fugues incorporated in *The Well-Tempered Clavier* was meant to provide one prelude and one fugue in every known key on that scale for instrumentalists to play. Bach's composition book was an early attempt to bring the standard scale into musical practice but it took a much longer time for composers and musicians to accept it. Not until 1800 was the scale accepted by musicians in Germany and not until 1850 in France and England. Only recently were the exact numerical frequencies (e.g., 440 vibrations per second for the A above middle C) universally set. Thus, what skilled composers and keyboard tuners were able to do by ear, mathematics could confirm by calculation.

Doubling Time

Most people don't want to calculate twelfth or thirty-second roots of numbers all the time, so they often are involved in finding various kinds of benchmarks for everyday use. One of these is "doubling time," the time it takes at a certain rate of growth for money or populations (or any other quantity) to double. Wouldn't you want to know how soon your investment would be worth twice as much, given compound interest, at a variety of interest rates? We already know from the population example that at 2 percent (a pretty poor interest rate), your money would double in 35 years. But how fast does it double at 8 percent (a more likely rate in the 1980s)? It turns out to be between 8 and 9 years; and at 15 percent, the interest rate during a few inflationary years in the late 1970s, money doubled in fewer than 5 years.

The shortcut for calculating doubling time is the following: Take the number 70, divide it by the growth rate in percent, and you will get the approximate time it takes any quantity to double. The number 70 is not as magical as it might appear. It derives from the algebra of log base e, 100 times the natural log of 2, or about 69. (Log base e is covered in elementary functions.)

Table 16

Interest Rate	Calculation	Doubling Time (in years)
2%	70/2	35
8%	70/8	8.7
15%	70/15	4.6

Braking Speed

Another example of the practical use of exponents is in calculating the distance it takes to stop a car traveling at a certain speed. You know from personal experience that a car takes longer to come to a halt if it is traveling at a higher speed. But do you know how much longer it takes? The numerical relationship between those two quantities—rate of speed and distance needed to come to a full stop—can be calculated, assuming that the car, the number and weight of the passengers, and the braking conditions remain the same.

What happens when you apply the brakes to a speeding car is that the kinetic energy—the energy of motion—is absorbed by the brakes and converted into heat. The kinetic energy of a moving car is defined as 1/2 the mass of the car times the square of its velocity.

$$\frac{1}{2}\,mv^2$$

Since according to the law of conservation of energy in physics the energy of the forward motion has to be completely dissipated into heat by the braking process, $(1/2)mv^2$ has to equal the braking force times the distance it takes for the car to come to a complete stop.

$$\frac{1}{2}\,mv^2 = \text{braking force } (F) \times \text{distance } (d)$$

Note that the velocity of the car (v) is always squared in this equation. Thus, speed is going to be critical in determining how much distance is needed to bring the car to a full stop.

In your drivers' education course, you probably had to memorize the fact that a car going 50 mph needs a braking distance of 133 feet to stop. This is true for a car with average weight. But because the velocity is squared in the formula above, the very same car going twice that speed (100 mph) is going to need 4 times the distance to stop ($133 \times 4 = 532$ feet, more than 1/10 of a mile). And the *time* it takes to come to a stop goes up correspondingly.

Tests made on actual drivers show that some additional time is required simply to react to danger ahead. Including reaction time in terms of distance, the total stopping distance in feet at various speeds is shown in Table 17.

Brightness and Distance

Another relationship that you can express in exponents is that between the brightness of a source of light and the distance between yourself and the light. As you walk toward the light, it will grow brighter—that you know from experience. But can mathematics (and physics) tell you how much brighter?

Table 17

Miles Per Hour	Reaction Distance (in feet)	Braking Distance (in feet)	Total Stopping Distance (in feet)
25	27.5	33	60.5
40	44.0	81	125.0
55	60.5	167	227.5
65	71.5	252	323.5
70	77.0	304	381.0

The following formula describes a relationship between light, brightness, and distance in terms of what is called the *inverse square*.

$$\text{Illumination} = \frac{\text{Source Intensity}}{r^2} \qquad \text{where } r = \text{distance}$$

The use of r to designate distance in the inverse square rule is an example of how subtle notation can be. You might expect d to represent distance; but in this instance, the distance from the light source should be thought of as a kind of radius from the source to the edges of an imaginary sphere. Hence r is used for radial distance.

As you double the distance between yourself and the light source, as you move from a distance of, say, 1 to 2 yards, the brightness of the light will diminish by 1/4 because the same amount of light has to be spread over an area 4 times as large (Figure 35).

Figure 35

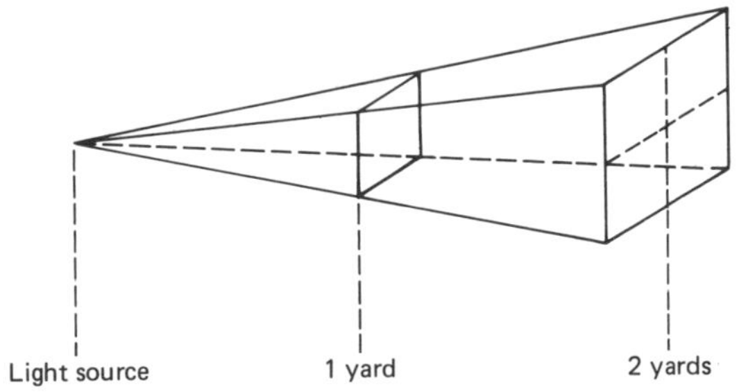

Light source   1 yard   2 yards

Similarly, if you halve the distance between yourself and the light source, the brightness will *increase* fourfold. If you think of the light moving through space like the ray of light illustrated in Figure 35, you can see why brightness has to increase and/or diminish by a factor of 4 as you halve or double the distance between yourself and the light source.

The Powers of 2

In probability problems you frequently explore the effect of growth that occurs when the exponent itself grows. Think about tossing pennies. If you have 2 pennies to toss, there are 4 possible outcomes: 2 heads, 2 tails, 1 head/1 tail, and 1 tail/1 head. Without doing any tossing, can you calculate the number of possible outcomes if you had 4 pennies, 50 pennies, or 100 pennies?

The answer is that you can calculate the number of possible outcomes so long as you can manipulate exponents. Take 2 as the base number (because a penny has 2 sides, there are 2 possibilities each time you toss) and raise it to the second power to find out how many possible outcomes there are when you toss 2 pennies. Two raised to the second power—2^2—is 4 and, indeed, there are 4 possible outcomes from the toss of 2 pennies. Using the same logic for 4 pennies, raise 2 to the power of 4 and you can predict 16 different outcomes. For 50 pennies, 2^{50} will be all the possible outcomes of the toss.

A very common application of the powers of 2, as these increases are called, is in computer design. The only physical actions the computer can register are on/off alternatives, since the transistors within each microchip are either conducting or not conducting electricity at any one moment in time. A single computer microchip is made up of hundreds of thousands of these transistors. Each transistor is either on or off, the way each tossed penny lands either on heads or tails. For this reason, computer logic is "binary," so called because it is based on a number system having only 2 numbers, 1 and 0.

Just as the possible outcomes of n penny tosses is expressed as 2^n, so the number of states that n transistors can jointly represent will also be 2^n. The n in this expression is called a bit, standing for *bi*nary dig*it*. And the information that can be carried by n transistors is n bits. Eight bits is called a byte.

The Powers of 10

Writing Large Numbers

Scientists and mathematicians rarely write out large numbers. They prefer scientific notation, a system of writing numbers based on the powers of 10.

$$10^0 = 1$$
$$10^1 = 10$$
$$10^2 = 100$$
$$10^3 = 1,000$$
$$10^4 = 10,000$$
$$10^5 = 100,000$$
$$10^6 = 1,000,000, \text{ and so on.}$$

When a more specific number is called for, such as 856,000, it is written in scientific notation as 8.56×10^5.

$$8.56 \times 10^5 = 8.56 \times 100,000 = 856,000$$

Once you are used to these conventions, it is easier to deal with large numbers and you are less prone to error. You will also gain an understanding of the expression *orders of magnitude*. Values that differ in exponents of 10 are described as having different orders of magnitude, meaning they are substantially different, not just plus or minus a few.

In the previous example of population growth, the figures were given in numerals and words.

Year	Total Population
1950	2.51 billion
1982	4.6 billion

A demographer would write this as follows:

1950	2.51×10^9
1982	$4.6 \ \times 10^9$

In this particular instance, using scientific notation doesn't save any time or space, but it does ensure universal understanding.

Writing Small Numbers

Very small numbers, much less than 1, are usually expressed as fractions or as decimals. With this in mind, you can see that very small numbers are just very large numbers written in the denominator. In the examples below, the larger the denominator, the smaller the value of the number given:

$$\frac{1}{13,645} > \frac{1}{500,670} > \frac{1}{2 \times 10^8}.$$

There is still another way to express very small numbers, not written as fractions, but as negative exponents of 10. You can go backward as well as forward with powers of 10.

$$10^2 \ = 100$$
$$10^1 \ = \ 10$$
$$10^0 \ = \ 1$$
$$10^{-1} = .10 \text{ or } \frac{1}{10}$$
$$10^{-2} = .01 \text{ or } \frac{1}{100}$$
$$10^{-3} = .001 \text{ or } \frac{1}{1,000}$$
$$\vdots$$
$$10^{-6} = .000001 \text{ or } \frac{1}{1,000,000}$$

For example, .000856 in scientific notation is written 8.56×10^{-4}.

An advantage to these expressions of large and small numbers is that they permit rapid visual calculations. To multiply $10^4 \times 10^6$, for example, merely add the exponents for a product of 10^{10}. By the same logic, to get $10^{10} \div 10^6$, subtract the exponents and get 10^4. This is an even more useful convention when the exponents are expressed in symbols as in $10^x \times 10^y = 10^{x + y}$.

Since scientific texts and even journals of popular science use scientific notation, it is important to become familiar with it as soon as possible.

How to Write in Scientific Notation

Most basic college math textbooks explain how to write numbers in scientific notation. Figure 36 shows one example, marked up by an avid math student. See if you can follow it. To take another example, 2^{50} expressed in scientific notation, figured out by means of a scientific calculator, is approximately 1.126×10^{15}.

How Fast Do Quantities Decline?

We have been looking at exponential *growth* in various guises. What about exponential *shrinkage?* Do quantities also decline at very rapid rates in the real world?

Let's take radioactive decay, the rate at which radioactive substances are naturally transformed. The measure of the rate of radioactive decay is a quantity known as the *half-life*. Half-life is the time required for half the original radioactive sample to undergo radioactive decay. This predictability is important for determining at what point it might be safe for technicians to reenter a contaminated area after an accident, or how long it would take for such an area to become habitable again.

If you know (as people now do) the half-life of a particular radioactive element, then you can figure out the time it will take for that material to decay. A substance with a half-life of 2 years, for example, will have 1/2 left after 2 years (1 half-life), 1/4 left after 4 years (2 half-lives), 1/8 left after 6 years (3 half-lives), 1/16 left after 8 years (4 half-lives), and 1/32 left after 10 years (5 half-lives). Radioactive decay follows the pattern of

$$\frac{1}{2^n}$$

where n is the number of half-lives and $1/2^n$ the fraction of the original sample that remains radioactive.

Say a substance has a half-life of 10 years. To find how much will remain undecayed after 150 years, we first have to calculate

Figure 36

I'm glad
this is in
Words.

> **To Express a Number Using Scientific Notation:**
>
> 1. First move the decimal point until it is to the imme-
>   diate right of the first nonzero digit.
>
> 2. Then multiply by 10^n or 10^{-n}, depending on whether
>   the decimal point was moved n places to the left or
>   to the right, respectively.

10 places

For example, to express the number 29,979,000,000 in scientific notation, first move the decimal point 10 places to the
left so that it's located between the 2 and the 9. Then multiply
by 10^{10}. The result is

$$29{,}979{,}000{,}000 = 2.9979000000 \times 10^{10}$$

or, more simply,

$$29{,}979{,}000{,}000 = 2.9979 \times 10^{10}$$

As additional examples we list the following numbers expressed in both ordinary and scientific notation. For practice
you should verify each conversion for yourself using our two-
step procedure.

$$55708 = 5.5708 \times 10^4 \to 55708 = 5.5708 \times 10^4$$
$$0.000099 = 9.9 \times 10^{-5} \to 0.000099 = 9.9 \times 10^{-5}$$
$$0.0000002 = 2 \times 10^{-7}$$

-5

$-7'$ $= 2 \times 10^{-7}$

---

the number of half-lives in 150 years by dividing 150 by 10 ($= 15$) and replacing n in the above equation with 15.

$$\frac{1}{2^{15}} = \frac{1}{32,768}$$ of the original material remains radioactive

Unfortunately, half-lives of some radioactive elements are in the 1,000- to 100,000-year range, so much much more will be left after 150 years than this example suggests. For a substance with a half-life of 15,000 years, $n = .01$ after 150 years:

$$\frac{1}{2^{.01}} = \frac{1}{1.007} = \text{approximately } .993.$$

Or, more than 99 percent of the original material remains radioactive. This is why the safe disposal of radioactive materials remains such a difficult and compelling task.

Large Numbers in Science

We have made passing reference to the importance of scientific notation in mathematics. It is also important in chemistry. One very large number that shows up early in chemistry is Avogadro's number, named after an early physical scientist, Amadeo Avogadro (1776–1856). Avogadro discovered that for all chemical elements, there is a constant number of molecules whose total mass is equal in grams to the atomic mass of their elements.

This is not an easy idea to follow without an example, so let's consider the hydrogen molecule with a molecular mass of 2, compared to the uranium molecule with a molecular mass of 238. According to Avogadro, there will be the same number of molecules in 2 grams of hydrogen as in 238 grams of uranium. That molecular quantity is called a *mole* and because it is such a large number, it is written as

$$6.02 \times 10^{23}.$$

So, according to Avogadro's rule, in 2 grams of hydrogen there are 6.02×10^{23} hydrogen molecules, and in 238 grams of uranium, there are 6.02×10^{23} uranium molecules.

Avogadro's number is gargantuan. If you were to write it out,

$$6.02 \times 10^{23}$$

would require 24 digits and would look like

$$602,000,000,000,000,000,000,000.$$

Imagine trying to study chemistry without scientific notation.

Sequences

Have you ever played a sequence-generating game? In this game, one player picks a sequence of numbers and challenges the other player to guess what number should follow. Given the sequence 2, 5, 10, 17, for example, the second player has to figure out the rule by which the sequence was generated. If you simply looked at the numbers 2, 5, 10, 17, you might not immediately recognize that they are part of an arithmetic sequence. But if you figured out the rule—starting with 1, square each successive integer and add 1—the fifth number in the sequence will have to be 26 ($5^2 + 1 = 26$).

In mathematics a sequence is any *nonrandom* succession of numbers that follows a certain rule. The simplest is our counting number system, which follows the rule that each successive term in the sequence is one more ($+1$) than the preceding term. The sequence 3, 6, 12, 24, 48 follows the rule that each succeeding term is twice the term that precedes it. The counting numbers are examples of an arithmetic sequence because the rule involves adding or subtracting a constant number to the previous term. The 3, 6, 12, 24 series is an example of a geometric sequence because it involves multiplying or dividing by a constant factor.

The rules for arithmetic and geometric sequences are usually obvious once you have three or more terms. Other kinds of sequences, however, are not so obvious, and rule-finding becomes an interesting mathematical task. But, however complicated, the principle behind all sequences is the same: Each successive term in the sequence must be generated by the same rule as the term before. If you can figure out the *rule* and you know which *position* in the sequence the term you are looking for occupies, then you can figure out what that term must be.

This is easier stated than done. Imagine you are asked to find the tenth term in a sequence when you are given a few of the initial terms but don't yet know the rule that generates the sequence.

Term:	First	Second	Third	Fourth	Fifth . . .
Value:	$\frac{1}{1}$	$\frac{1}{2}$	$\frac{1}{3}$	$\frac{1}{4}$	$\frac{1}{5}$ . . .

This seems to be a straightforward sequence generated by adding 1 to each denominator. Since the second term is 1/2 and the fourth term is 1/4, it seems reasonable to assume that the tenth term will be 1/10, and that, if the sequence went up that high, the two hundred thirty-third term would be 1/233. In other words, if you know the *position* of any term in this sequence (like tenth), you can correctly guess its value. You might want to know the last term in a finite sequence. If it is not given, mathematicians often use the letter N to denote the last term. So, by the same logic, in this sequence the last or Nth term would be $1/N$.

Term:	First	Second	Third	Fourth	Fifth . . .	Nth
Value:	$\frac{1}{1}$	$\frac{1}{2}$	$\frac{1}{3}$	$\frac{1}{4}$	$\frac{1}{5}$ . . .	$\frac{1}{N}$

This is a very important idea, more useful than it may at first appear. In any sequence governed by a constant rule, the *position* of a term in the sequence will be the key to figuring out its value.

This means that in order to generalize the rule for any particular sequence, we are going to have to find a way to express an *unspecified* position in the sequence. The first, second, third, and even the Nth positions in the sequence are specific. If we are going to be able to say something about *any* position in the sequence, we will need a term like the "any-th" position, and mathematicians have devised one: the "ith" term. Just as Nth stands for the last term in a finite sequence, so ith (pronounced eith) or jth or hth stands for the any-th term. In the sequence we have been looking at, the ith term would be written $1/i$.

Term:	First	Second	Third	Fourth . . .	ith . . .	Nth
Value:	$\frac{1}{1}$	$\frac{1}{2}$	$\frac{1}{3}$	$\frac{1}{4}$ . . .	$\frac{1}{i}$ . . .	$\frac{1}{N}$

This may seem unnecessarily abstract, but as you will see, having a generic ith makes it possible to express the rule of the sequence as well.

But first look at some more examples. Here is another sequence where the rule is not quite so easy to figure out simply by inspection.

Term:	First	Second	Third	Fourth ...	ith ...	Nth
Value:	$\dfrac{1}{2}$	$\dfrac{1}{5}$	$\dfrac{1}{10}$	$\dfrac{1}{17}$	?	?

What we are looking for is a rule or formula for a sequence that progresses from a starting point of 1/2 to 1/5 in the second position, 1/10 in the third position, and 1/17 in the fourth position. By trial and error we can find the rule that generates this series. Take the position of a term (first, second, third, Nth, etc.) and square this number. Add 1. Put the new number in the denominator of a fraction whose numerator is 1. Now you have the next term in the sequence. Look again at the sequence above. For the second term, following this rule, take the position number 2, square it ($2^2 = 4$), and add 1 to get the denominator.

$$\frac{1}{2^2 + 1} = \frac{1}{5}$$

For the third term, take the position number 3, square it ($3^2 = 9$), add 1, and you have the denominator for the third term.

$$\frac{1}{3^2 + 1} = \frac{1}{10}$$

The fourth term is generated in the same way.

$$\frac{1}{4^2 + 1} = \frac{1}{17}$$

The same rule works for the Nth term. Take the position number N, square it (N^2), and add one to get the denominator for the Nth term.

$$\frac{1}{N^2 + 1}$$

Any term in the sequence can then be expressed using *i*. If

$$\frac{1}{N^2 + 1}$$

is the last (*N*th term) in that sequence, then by the same logic,

$$\frac{1}{i^2 + 1}$$

represents *any* term in the same sequence. And this is precisely where *i* becomes very useful. If we knew the term we were looking for was the twenty-first term, we could find its value simply by substituting 21 for *i* in the general formula:

$$\frac{1}{i^2 + 1} = \frac{1}{21^2 + 1} = \frac{1}{441 + 1} = \frac{1}{442}.$$

Before turning to some common applications of the concept of the *i*th term, let's look at one more sequence to demonstrate how *i* is used in the rule that governs the sequence.

Suppose we had the following sequence:

Term:	First	Second	Third	Fourth . . . *i*th . . . *N*th
Value:	3	9	27	81 ? ?

By inspection we can see that in this sequence the number 3 is raised to ever-increasing exponents.

Term:	First	Second	Third	Fourth . . . *i*th . . . *N*th
Value:	3	9	27	81 ? ?
	3^1	3^2	3^3	3^4 3^i 3^N

To express the rule most succinctly we must find the value of the *i*th term. Since the *position* in the sequence is the *power* to which 3 is raised to generate the sequence, the rule for this sequence can be expressed as

$$3^i.$$

To calculate the value of any term in the sequence, the rule obliges us to take the position of that term and make it the exponent of 3.

To find the value of the twenty-first term in that sequence, substitute 21 for i in the rule 3^i. Then 3^{21} is the twenty-first term in that sequence.

Summing Sequences

Summing numbers is a considerably slower process than working with exponentials and factorials. And if you have to sum a very long sequence of mathematical expressions by hand or even with the aid of a calculator, addition will be extremely time-consuming. Try the following addition on your calculator: Sum $1 + 2 + 3 + 4$ up to 100. You can imagine how tedious it would be to add longer and even more complicated sequences. But there is a way to shorten the process, a way that brings us to an important and interesting set of operations in mathematics.

If you write out the numbers you have to add up *twice,* first in one direction (say, 1, 2, 3, 4, 5), and then in the reverse direction (5, 4, 3, 2, 1), you will notice an interesting result.

1	2	3	4	5
5	4	3	2	1
6	6	6	6	6

Every sum adds up to 6. If you then multiply that common sum (6) by the *number* of terms in the sequence (5), you will get 30, which turns out to be *twice* the sum of the sequence ($1 + 2 + 3 + 4 + 5 = 15$). Thirty *has* to be twice the total because we have written out and summed the numbers 1, 2, 3, 4, and 5 *twice,* once forward, once backward. Herein lies the germ of an idea for short-cutting the process of adding long arithmetic sequences.

In summing a short, simple sequence such as 1, 2, 3, 4, 5, standard addition is the easiest and quickest method. But suppose you wanted to sum a longer sequence, such as the integers from 1 to 25. You can apply this principle without summing the entire sequence written out forward and backward. In working with the arithmetic sequence, you can assume that if the first and last terms of the sequence add up to 26 ($1 + 25 = 26$), the second term added to the next-to-last term and the third term added to the third from the last term, etc., will all sum to 26.

1	2	3	4 ... 22	23	24	25
25	24	23	22 ... 4	3	2	1
26	26	26	26 26	26	26	26

There are 25 terms in this sequence and the common sum is 26. Using your calculator, you need only multiply 26 (the common sum) by 25 (the number of terms in the sequence). That operation will give you twice the sum of the sequence and dividing by 2 will get you the correct answer.

$$25 \times 26 = 650$$

$$650 \div 2 = 325$$

$$\text{The sum of 1 to 25} = 325$$

If you add the integers from 1 to 25 on your calculator you will confirm that the sum of this series (a series is the consecutive adding of the terms of a sequence) is correct. You can see how much easier and less tedious it is to use the shortcut than to add each of those integers in turn. This is a shortcut that will work for all arithmetic series:

- Add the first and last terms in the series.

- Multiply that sum by the number of terms in the series.

- Divide that total by 2.

It is said that Carl Friedrich Gauss (1777–1855), one of the most creative mathematicians of all time, was 10 years old when he came upon this solution to the problem of summing series. The story is told that when Gauss was a pupil in elementary school, it was hard for his teacher to keep him from being bored. One day, in desperation, the teacher gave Gauss an assignment that the teacher assumed would take the young boy a long time to finish. Gauss was told to add all the integers from 1 to 100. In no time at all, to his teacher's astonishment, Gauss had the answer: 5,050. He had figured out the system just described for summing series.

If young Gauss was smart enough to figure out this system, you can be sure he was also smart enough to figure out that he did not have to write out all 100 integers twice. He merely did a sampling of those additions, recognized that there was a common sum (101) and proceeded to multiply that common sum by the number of terms and then to divide by 2.

Sequences and series appear so often in mathematics and mathematical applications that a standard notation has been devised to express the idea of *summing series*. This notation is based on the principle of summing devised so long ago by Gauss, and involves some new symbols.

$$\sum_{i=1}^{100}$$

$i = 1$ means substitute 1 where it says i in the general expression to get the value of the first term to be added; then make $i = 2$, $i = 3$, and so on until $i = 100$. Σ is the Greek capital letter S or Sigma (for sum). So the next and last step is to add all the i terms in the series.

Imagine that you were asked to sum the infinite series, $1/2 + 1/5 + 1/10 + 1/17$. . . to the 100th term in this series. This is the series whose rule we found to be

$$\frac{1}{i^2 + 1}.$$

This particular summation would be expressed in summation notation as

$$\sum_{i=1}^{100} \frac{1}{i^2 + 1}.$$

Note that the i to the right is now part of an expression representing the rule. The i below means start with the first term. The 100 above means end with the 100th term. Now everything you need to know to specify the sum is contained in this expression.

By the same logic, if we were to sum the series $3 + 9 + 27 + 81$ . . . , to the 100th term in that series, whose rule we found to be 3^i, the summation expression would be written

$$\sum_{i=1}^{100} 3^i.$$

You can see now how critical the i term is. Without it, there would be no way to express the general rule either of a sequence or a series.

To summarize, the summation expression has to have two parts.

1. The sum sign with its beginning and end indicators:

$$\sum_{i=1}^{N} \quad \sum_{i=0}^{k}.$$

2. The sequence-generating rule, always written to the right of the sum sign and in terms of i (or j or k or any other symbol).

$$\sum_{i=1}^{n} 3^i \quad \sum_{i=1}^{100} \frac{1}{i^2 + 1}.$$

If you wanted to describe these expressions in words, you would say:

> The sum of the quantities 3 raised to the ith power as i goes from 1 to n.

> The sum of the quantities 1 divided by $i^2 + 1$ as i goes from 1 to 100.

Applying the Law of Odd Numbers

One pattern that reveals itself when you begin to sum integers is the so-called law of odd numbers. Take a sequence made up of odd integers beginning with 1: 1, 3, 5, 7, 9, 11. Add them and you will find that they sum to sequential squares.

$$1 + 3 = 4 \quad (2^2)$$
$$1 + 3 + 5 = 9 \quad (3^2)$$
$$1 + 3 + 5 + 7 = 16 \quad (4^2)$$
$$1 + 3 + 5 + 7 + 9 = 25 \quad (5^2)$$
$$1 + 3 + 5 + 7 + 9 + 11 = 36 \quad (6^2)$$

This relationship was known before Galileo Galilei (1564–1642), but he was the first to see that the sum of odd numbers corresponds to the behavior of falling bodies. Galileo was attempting to understand gravity quantitatively. He carefully measured the distance an object falls within a certain interval of time and noticed that there was a constant acceleration in the rate of fall. The object fell a certain distance during the first time interval, a greater distance during the second, a still greater distance during the third, and so on.

Galileo reasoned that there was a numerical pattern in the fall, one that followed the law of odd numbers. If the body fell 1 unit during the first time interval, it fell 3 units during the next, and 5 during the next, and so on. Since the total distance fallen could be calculated by adding these various distances, Galileo got the sequence that we just achieved by adding 1, 1 + 3, 1 + 3 + 5, 1 + 3 + 5 + 7, and 1 + 3 + 5 + 7 + 9, and he recognized these sums as squares (4, 9, 16, 25). The distance a body falls under the influence of gravity, Galileo discovered, is proportional to the square of the time elapsed during the fall; or, as we express it today, bodies fall (on earth) at the rate of 32 feet per second squared, written 32 ft/sec^2.

Estimating and Approximating

One of the many advantages of getting comfortable with large and small numbers is that you can begin to employ new powers of estimation within appropriate limits. In many real-life applications, exact answers remain as important as when you were struggling with your first arithmetic facts. Still, it will sometimes be very useful to be able to do back-of-the-envelope calculations, as estimates and approximations are called, both as a check on your work and to avoid tedious calculations until they are absolutely needed. When working with a calculator, it is especially important to do estimates before plugging in all of the numbers. Your fingers can slip. You can forget a term. You can push the wrong sign. But if you have already estimated an answer, you will realize if an error has occurred somewhere in your calculation. Also, you will never be embarrassed by making errors of magnitude, that is, coming up with answers that are 10 times or 1/10 what they are supposed to be.

Best of all, estimating and approximating can give you a feeling of *control* over your mathematics . . . and over your life. Once you remove yourself from the details of a problem and do a rough estimate of the general range of the likely answer, you will feel more secure as you work out the problem, certain that you will not end up too far off. Also, that broad overview of the task is surely going to help you get started, and keep you from getting bogged down. Here, too, is where scientific notation can come in very handy and where shortcuts, like knowing doubling time, can be of use. Here is where competence with exponentials and the ability to do a quick sketch of an equation on a graph pay off.

Control over your mathematics and control over your life are two realistic goals you can achieve.

Chapter

6

Equalities and Inequalities

From Arithmetic to Algebra

Algebra represents a great leap forward in mathematical abstraction. This may not be immediately obvious because, in the beginning, you continue to do algebra arithmetically simply using x and y as unknowns. Take the following example.

You have a certain amount of money. You triple that amount and then your aunt gives you $5 more. If you end up with $65, how much money did you start with?

If you set up the problem as follows, x is the initial amount of money.

$$x = \frac{\$65 - \$5}{3}$$

$$x = \frac{\$60}{3}$$

$$x = \$20$$

Although this looks like an algebraic manipulation, you are actually just turning the problem into an arithmetic problem. But if, instead, you were to proceed by representing the initial sum of money with the symbol x and then writing a mathematical statement (an equation) involving x that will lead you logically to an answer, you will have taken the first step across the divide that separates algebra from arithmetic. The equation will now look like:

$$3x + \$5 = \$65$$
$$3x = \$65 - \$5$$
$$3x = \$60$$
$$x = \$20.$$

Translating the problem statement directly into a mathematical expression gives you a powerful new tool for solving far more complex problems than this one.

Understanding Variables

The next step in moving from arithmetic to algebra occurs when you realize that if your aunt had given you an unknown quantity of dollars instead of the specific $5, you would have been able to adjust your original equation to represent the two unknowns like this:

$$3x + y = \$65.$$

This equation, as you may know, doesn't have a single solution but rather an *infinite* number of *pairs* of solutions because x and y vary with one another. When x and y are not unique unknowns but can take on a variety of numerical values, they are called variables and it is as variables that you will see them used most of the time in mathematics.

As you have already learned, equations and the various rules for manipulating them comprise the bulk of elementary and intermediate algebra. But most relationships in the real world do *not* conform to the exact relationships of equality. Most quantities are not exactly equal to other quantities but are, rather, larger than or smaller than something else and have to be dealt with by statements of inequality, as in the following examples.

$x > 65$ meaning x is greater than 65

$x < 65$ meaning x is less than 65

$x \geq 65$ meaning x is greater than or equal to 65

$x \leq 65$ meaning x is less than or equal to 65

Inequalities

In this chapter you are going to explore some powerful strategies for handling inequalities. These strategies form the basis of a branch of applied mathematics called linear programming, which is the single most widely used tool today in solving planning problems in business and industry.

What makes the mathematics of inequalities and the techniques of linear programming so relevant is that they provide a way of making "optimal decisions," that is, the best and most rational decisions within certain real-life constraints. In mathematics, a constraint usually limits the size of a number or a function. In the real world, a constraint limits some important quantity and is usually expressed as a statement of inequality.

The amount of money you have in your bank account at any one time, to take one real-life example, is a constraint on your spending. Without going into debt, you can only spend an amount *equal to* or *less than* your bank balance. Constraints in other areas may be at the lower end; for example, to maintain your right to a student loan, you may take 12 or more credit-hours per semester, but not fewer.

In the mathematics you'll be looking at in this chapter, the real-life constraint will be expressed as an inequality and the objective will be to maximize something that you want, like profit, or to minimize something you don't want, like cost; in short, to *optimize,* to make the best possible combination of resources, whatever they might be.

If inequalities are so important, why are they not emphasized more in high school? One reason is that the high school mathematics curriculum was traditionally designed to prepare you for the physical sciences, which are not primarily concerned with problems of *optimization under constraints*. The physical sciences strive for *exact* predictions that emerge out of relationships of equality between time, velocity, and acceleration, for example, in physics; or the amount of the final product that results from a chemical reaction. The essential conservation of mass and energy in the natural world virtually precludes inequalities because every bit of mass or energy that existed before a physical event took place has to be accounted for afterward.

Scientists are so accustomed to dealing with equalities that when one inequality showed up in beta decay during early experiments with radioactivity, physicists such as Wolfgang Pauli and Enrico Fermi were forced to hypothesize, long before they had any hard evidence for this, that there *had* to be an undetectable particle in the process of beta decay to make the total amount of energy at the end of the decay process equal to what was there before. Fermi was so certain of the particle's existence that he gave it a name, the *neutrino,* almost 20 years before it was finally discovered by someone else.

If equalities prepare you for the mathematics used in physics, chemistry, and the biological sciences, inequalities and optimization procedures are most pertinent to management. As business enterprises have become larger and business decision making more complex, techniques have been developed for handling constraints in the form of inequalities in order to optimize either production or profits.

Linking Algebra and Geometry

The techniques for solving management problems are essentially algebraic, but they have been considerably enriched by geometric insights that allow constraints to be "seen" as areas or volumes in space, and the "right decision" to be conceptualized as a *corner point* where several lines or faces meet. You have already encountered a few of the links between algebra and geometry, but you may not have been aware of them as links at the time. The first is the number line on which zero is located at the center with positive numbers to the right and negative numbers to the left (see Figure 37).

This geometric visualization of real numbers illustrates the con-

Figure 37

Figure 37

tinuity between negative and positive numbers and the one-to-one correspondence between a particular number and a particular point on a line.

A second link occurs when you begin graphing equations. In order to think about a location in two-dimensional space, two number lines, one called the x-axis, the other the y-axis, can be drawn perpendicular to one another so that they cross at the zero point on both (Figure 38).

Apart from these examples, algebra and geometry are usually taught as if they dealt with two very different aspects of mathe-

Figure 38

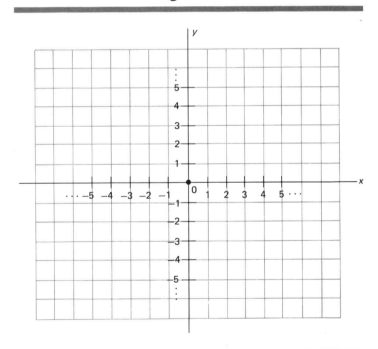

matics: geometry as a way of handling forms, shapes, and angles of two- and three-dimensional objects in space; algebra as symbolic in its language and sequential (not visual) in its logic. Geometry is taught around a body of proofs, while algebra is thought to be computational, structured around certain word problems and their solutions. Yet algebra and geometry are not separate subjects but rather two facets of some of the most profound and interesting relationships in mathematics and, as you will see in this chapter, both contribute significantly to the theory and practice of linear programming.

The first person in history who properly understood the connection between algebra and geometry was the seventeenth-century French thinker René Descartes (1596–1650), who left his mark on both philosophy and mathematics. Descartes's books *The Geometry* and *The Discourse on Method* showed how geometry and algebra are intertwined. To begin to appreciate his contribution, let's start with a review of the graphing of *equalities* and then proceed to see how *inequalities* can be treated geometrically as well.

Figure 39

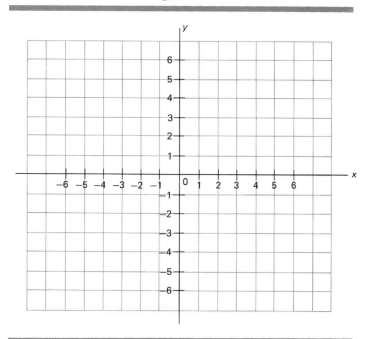

The Cartesian "Address System"

Two ready-made images for what are now called the Cartesian coordinates (after Descartes) are latitude and longitude on a map. To find a single point on a graph (an address) to correspond to a pair of values for x and y, we can think about values along the x-axis as various longitudes and values along the y-axis as various latitudes. (One could do the reverse, but by convention, x is usually the horizontal axis and y the vertical.) Since x and y values can be positive or negative in algebra, x points are drawn "east" (positive) or "west" (negative) on the horizontal x-axis; y values are drawn "north" (positive) and "south" (negative) on the vertical y-axis. The result is a *coordinate* system in the plane (Figure 39).

What makes this "address system" so powerful is that each pair of values of x and y corresponds to a unique location in the plane. For example, the pairs of numbers below will correspond to the points plotted in Figure 40.

$$A: x = \quad 2, \quad y = \quad 3$$
$$B: x = -5, \quad y = \quad 2$$
$$C: x = -4, \quad y = -3$$
$$D: x = \quad 5, \quad y = -4$$

The pair of numbers such as 2 (for x) and 3 (for y) associated with a particular geometric point are the *pair of coordinates* (also called the *ordered pair*) for that point. So, the coordinates of Point A in Figure 40 are $x = 2$, $y = 3$, usually abbreviated as (2,3) with the x value given first. For Point B, $(-5,2)$. For Point C, $(-4,-3)$, and for Point D $(5,-4)$.

Graphing Equalities

Let's plot just two examples of linear equations on the Cartesian plane. The first is $x + y = 60$. There are an infinite number of solutions to this equation, which can be expressed as ordered pairs, such as:

Figure 40

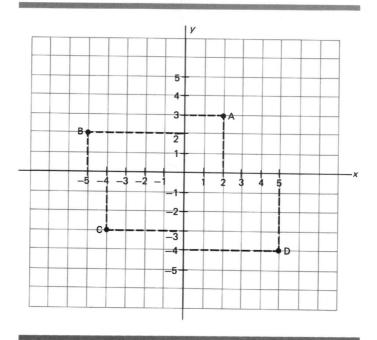

$$x = 10, \quad y = 50$$
$$x = 15, \quad y = 45$$
$$x = 30, \quad y = 30$$
$$x = 59, \quad y = 1$$
$$x = 100, \quad y = -40$$

If you plot the points associated with these ordered pairs, you discover that they lie on a straight line, as you can see by drawing a line through each point (Figure 41). This straight line represents *all* of the pairs of solutions to the equation $x + y = 60$.

Now look at the linear equation $3x + y = 90$ (Figure 42). Some of the ordered pairs that satisfy this equation are

$$x = 10, \quad y = 60$$
$$x = 15, \quad y = 45.$$

Figure 41

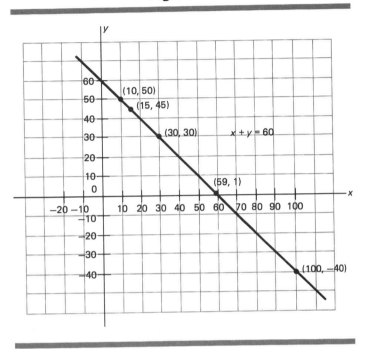

When you graph the two equations you get two straight lines with different slopes. When you put the two together the two straight lines intersect exactly at the point where $x = 15$ and $y = 45$. This ordered pair, then, is said to satisfy both equations. That point on the graph is designated I (Figure 43).

$$x + y = 60$$
$$3x + y = 90$$

Visualizing Equations

While graphing equations does not ordinarily give you exact quantitative solutions to problems, graphs do give you a sense of the behavior of different functions because their geometry is always quite distinctive. Linear equations, the kinds we just plotted, are

Figure 42

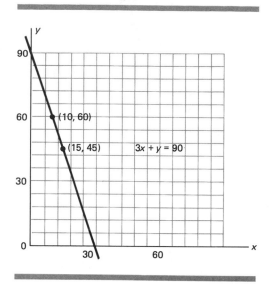

always straight lines. Equations having exponents greater than one are represented by curves. A quick look at a certain equation will tell the experienced math student whether the curve will rise or fall, whether it will be symmetrical or asymmetrical, whether it will oscillate or bend, roughly how steep its climb or descent will be.

Once you are familiar with these geometric curves you will be more confident in plotting and solving algebraic equations. Figures 44–48 show a few of the most basic curves together with the equations they represent.

Talking Mathematics

These geometric forms and the equations they represent have become part of our spoken language, largely because they provide a useful visual shorthand by which to describe change. When people speak about the path of a ball thrown into the air, they visualize the parabolic curve (see p. 125). "Exponential" means very rapid growth or decay.

However, some terms in mathematics have entirely different meanings than they have in ordinary use and some have more than one meaning. "Normal," for example, means "perpendicular" in

Figure 43

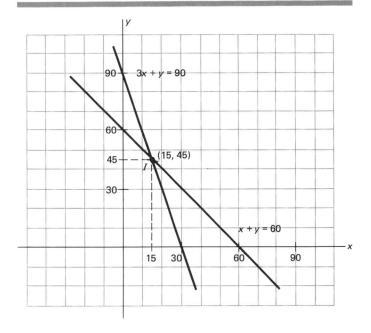

Figure 44. Circle

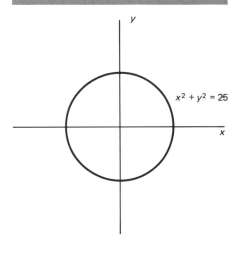

Figure 45. Hyperbola

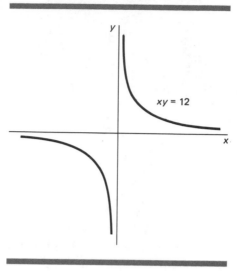

$xy = 12$

physics, but in statistics a "normal distribution" is a bell-shaped curve. Neither term has anything to do with the meanings of "normal" in everyday English ("ordinary," "common," or "mentally healthy"). But terms like "slope of the curve" and "hyperbolic"

Figure 46. Normal Distribution Curve

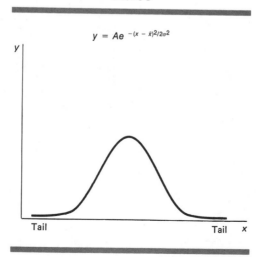

$y = Ae^{-(x - \bar{x})^2/2\sigma^2}$

Tail   Tail   x

Figure 47. Parabola

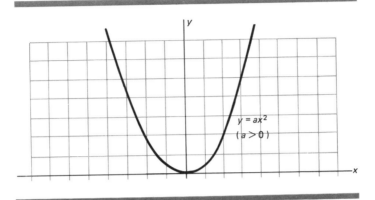

Figure 48. Sine Curve and Cosine Curve

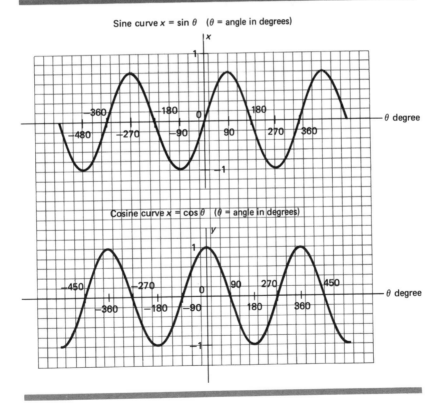

Figure 49

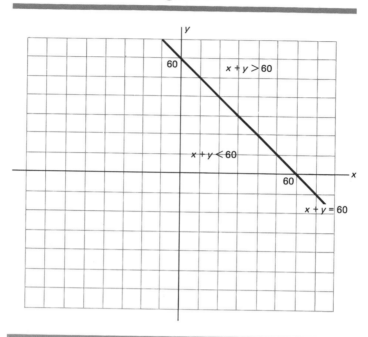

have now entered our spoken language, and anyone unfamiliar with these technical terms will be at a professional disadvantage. Familiarity with analytic geometry opens the way not only to more advanced scientific and mathematical reasoning, but to a more powerful vocabulary as well.

Graphing Inequalities

Linear equations are represented as straight lines on the Cartesian axes, and linear inequalities are represented by areas, bounded by straight lines, called *regions*. If the straight line on Figure 49 represents the equation $x + y = 60$, then all the points that are *above* the line must represent $x + y > 60$ and all the points *below*

Figure 50

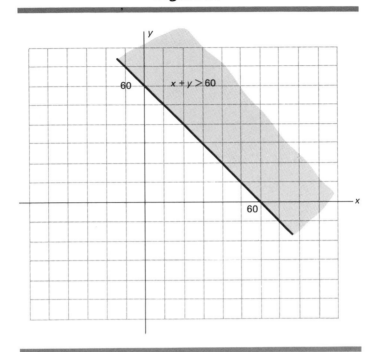

that line represent $x + y < 60$. The logic is that to go from the $x + y < 60$ region to the $x + y > 60$ region you will have to pass across the line representing $x + y = 60$.

If we were to shade in the region that is above the line $x + y = 60$, we would have a graphic representation of the inequality $x + y > 60$ (Figure 50). Similarly, if we were to shade in the region below the line $x + y = 60$, we would have a graphic representation of the inequality $x + y < 60$ (Figure 51). By the same logic, we can graph the inequality $3x + y < 90$ (Figure 52).

You can graph algebraic inequalities quite as easily as algebraic equalities, but they will be represented by shaded *regions* rather than by *points* on a straight line.

Suppose you wanted to "solve" a system of two linear inequalities. When you tried to solve a system of two linear equalities, you looked for the point that was common to both straight lines

Figure 51

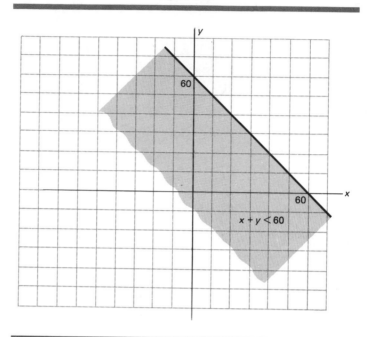

60

60 — x

$x + y < 60$

(see p. 123). In solving a system of inequalities, you will be looking for an area bounded by straight lines. In the real world, quantities of goods such as coal, steel, or soybeans cannot be minus quantities, so real-life problems generally add two other sets of inequalities as constraints: x and y are assumed to be equal to or greater than zero.

In Figure 53, we have the graph of a solution to a system of linear inequalities that would be written as follows in algebra.

$x + y \leq 60$ meaning $x + y$ is less than or equal to 60

$3x + y \leq 90$ meaning $3x + y$ is less than or equal to 90

$x \geq 0$ meaning x is greater than or equal to 0

$y \geq 0$ meaning y is greater than or equal to 0

The logic involved in solving systems of inequalities is the same as that used in solving systems of equalities. The ordered pairs (x,y) that satisfy all the inequalities simultaneously correspond to all the

Figure 52

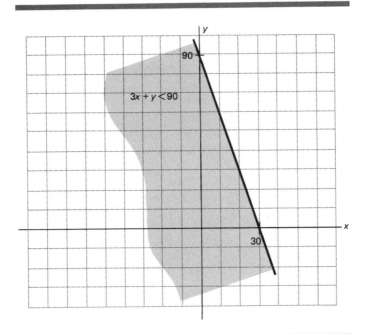

$3x + y < 90$

Figure 53

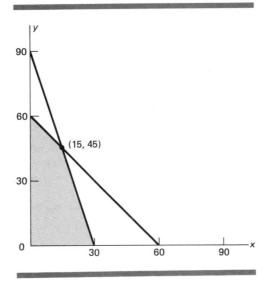

(15, 45)

points that lie in the shaded regions. In the graph (Figure 53), the solution of the system of inequalities corresponds to all points that lie below both straight lines and are bounded by the positive x and positive y axes.

The solution to this system of four inequalities is said to be represented by all the points that lie within the bounded region of the plane, which is in the form of a polygon. Since all the points within this particular polygon will satisfy the constraints expressed by the four inequalities that we have graphed, this polygon is called a *constraint polygon* and is the fundamental concept in linear programming.

Linear Programming and Management Science

You know from your reading of history that technology was the engine that drove the Industrial Revolution in its early stages. New forms of energy, new products, and new modes of transportation multiplied human productivity many times over between 1780 and about 1930. Two hundred years ago it took 75 percent of a nation's workforce to feed its population. Today, only a small portion of the workforce in the industrial world is engaged in growing, packaging, and distributing food.

After the first third of this century, technological innovation seemed to have leveled off, and business leaders, for the first time, began to pay some attention to improving management and organization as a means of increasing productivity. By improving organization and planning under existing technological conditions, they hoped to continue the upward trend in efficiency and productivity. Interestingly, some of the initial impetus for this new thinking came out of the Soviet Union, which in the 1920s and 1930s was desperately trying to industrialize a very backward economy. At the time, it seemed even more imperative to Soviet planners than to our own to whittle down waste and inefficiency in order to meet the goals of their various economic plans.

Thus, it is not altogether surprising that the first attempts to *mathematize* organizational management and planning took place in the planned economy of the USSR. L. V. Kantorovich, a Soviet economist, mathematician, and industrial consultant, proposed the first linear programming approach to solving management problems as early as 1939.

Linear programming (not to be confused with computer programming) involves the scheduling of production, distribution, and transportation of labor, materials, and products in a factory or in an industry as a whole.

Kantorovich attempted to make the scheduling of manufacturing assignments in Soviet plants more scientific by taking into consideration such constraints as the plant's production capacity, its distance from the nearest rail head, its distance from its suppliers, the quality of its workforce, how many hours its machines could go without needing maintenance—in short *everything* that went into production. Today, these *scheduling constraints* for tasks as varied as airline routing, military maneuvers, and even exam scheduling in universities are fed into large computers. But at the time Kantorovich began to think about linear scheduling, neither the concepts nor the mathematical formulas were readily at hand.

Then, in the 1940s, two Americans, the economist T. C. Koopmans and the mathematician George Dantzig, made linear programming both more elegant and more usable. Dantzig's breakthrough was the simplex method of solving linear programming problems in which the constraints run into the hundreds and thousands. Linear programming today is considered so important for modern management that in 1975 Kantorovich and Koopmans were awarded the Nobel Prize in economics for their work. (Dantzig did not share in the prize because he is primarily a mathematician and there is no Nobel Prize in mathematics.)

Linear programming is employed where there is a series of individual but related activities that have to share a scarce resource such as money, material, or time. The mathematization of the situation permits a manager to select a schedule—some kind of sequence of events—that will optimize the process. Not surprisingly, large organizations with many complicated activities to schedule were the first customers for linear programming. Dantzig began applying his new technology to the peace-time air force immediately after World War II. The U.S. Air Force wanted to maximize the quality and amount of flight training with the fewest number of flights. The mathematization of the problem and Dantzig's method gave them the optimum they wanted.

By 1951, linear programming had spread to the civilian sector and today it is hard to find an industry where linear programming isn't being used. As you may have noticed from this brief history, linear programming has grown up in the same era as computers. It is estimated that 25 percent of all computer time assigned to business problem solving (as compared with routine activities such as payroll and inventory) is taken up with linear programming. This is but one indication of the importance of linear programming and the value to you of finding out more about it.

The following is a straightforward linear programming problem that will give you a "feel" for the subject. We will approach the problem by means of geometry, though you should be aware at the outset that problems in more than two or three dimensions cannot be solved this way. Linear programming problems today are solved algebraically, but they rest on insights derived from the kind of geometry we will be doing in the next section—another example of the links between algebra and geometry.

The Farmer's Dilemma

Here is a typical linear programming problem in two dimensions:

A farmer is trying to decide how many acres should be devoted to growing corn and how many acres should be planted with soybeans. There are a total of 60 acres on his farm. Each acre of corn requires 3 gallons of herbicide, while each acre of soybeans requires only 1 gallon of the same chemical. For ecological reasons, only 90 gallons of herbicide can be used in total on the farm.

The farmer estimates that after all costs are deducted, each acre of corn yields a net profit of $60, while each acre of soybeans yields a net profit of $50. The decision to be made is: How should the land be allocated if the farmer wants to maximize total net profit?

Let's think about this problem in general. The farmer's goal is to realize the largest possible profit. The profit will depend on two quantities—the number of acres of corn planted and the number of acres of soybeans. The challenge is to choose values of these two quantities that *maximize* profit. But we are not free to choose these values arbitrarily. We must operate within the two constraints—the acreage limit and the herbicide limit.

The problem can be restated this way:

Objective: Allocate land to maximize profit

Decisions to be made:
  1. How many acres of corn should be planted?
  2. How many acres of soybeans should be planted?

Constraints:
  a. Total acreage planted cannot exceed 60 acres.
  b. Total amount of herbicide used cannot exceed 90 gallons.

Translation Into Algebra

Let's try to translate the problem into algebraic terms. We don't know the number of acres of corn and soybeans that the farmer will eventually decide to plant. Those are the unknowns in the problem. So let's call the number of acres of corn x and the number of acres of soybeans y. Since each acre of corn yields $60, the total profit from corn is: $60 multiplied by the number of acres of corn, or $60x$. Similarly, since each acre of soybeans planted shows a profit of $50, the total profit from soybeans can be expressed as: $50 multiplied by the number of acres of soybeans, or $50y$. The total profit, then, is the sum of the two preceding expressions.

- Profit from corn: $60x$

- Profit from soybeans: $50y$

- Total profit: $60x + 50y = P$ (profit)

The objective, "allocate land to maximize profit," becomes the mathematical problem: "Choose values of x and y to maximize the value of P in the equation $60x + 50y = P$."

Now, we have to look at the first constraint. We cannot assign x and y just any values, because there is a herbicide-use restriction and certain limits on how many total acres he can plant. So, the next task is to rewrite the constraints in the language of mathematics. Since the total acreage planted must be less than or equal to 60 acres, we express this constraint as an inequality:

$$\text{total acreage planted} \leq 60.$$

The total acreage planted equals the number of acres of corn *plus* the number of acres of soybeans, so the first constraint can be written:

$$x + y \leq 60 \quad \text{(acres)}.$$

The second constraint has to do with the allowable amount of herbicide, which can also be expressed as an inequality:

$$\begin{matrix}\text{number of gallons} \\ \text{used for corn}\end{matrix} + \begin{matrix}\text{number of gallons} \\ \text{used for soybeans}\end{matrix} \leq 90.$$

Each acre of corn requires 3 gallons of herbicide and each acre of soybeans, 1 gallon, so this inequality can be restated as below.

$$3\left(\frac{\text{gallons}}{\text{acre}}\right) \times x\,(\text{acres}) + 1\left(\frac{\text{gallons}}{\text{acre}}\right) \times y\,(\text{acres}) \leq 90\,(\text{gallons})$$

$$3x + y \leq 90$$

We have succeeded in translating the objective and the two constraints into algebraic notation. We have also translated the outcome into the equation $60x + 50y = P$. Our next mathematical task is to decide on values of x and y that (1) satisfy the two inequality constraints and (2) make the profit (P) as large as possible. There are two additional constraints that are tacitly understood in our problem dealing with land and herbicide. Negative acres of land are not possible in the real world. Hence:

$$x \,(\text{acres of corn}) \geq 0$$

$$y \,(\text{acres of soybeans}) \geq 0.$$

So, the farmer's problem is expressed in algebra as follows: Choose values of x and y so as to maximize P in the equation $60x + 50y = P$ subject to the following four constraints:

$$x + y \leq 60 \text{ acres}$$

$$3x + y \leq 90 \text{ gallons}$$

$$x \geq 0$$

$$y \geq 0.$$

Translation Into Geometry

Now that we have translated the problem from a question of agriculture into a question of algebra, the solution will be found by graphing the inequalities geometrically. We need to be able to visualize all of the possible corn-soybean allocations that satisfy the constraints because we will eventually want to *search* for the one

Figure 54

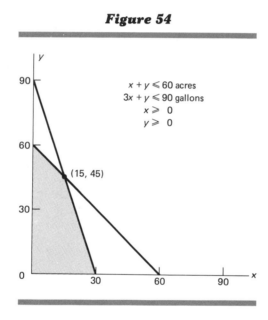

solution—among all those possible—that maximizes profit. As you can see (Figure 54) this particular system of inequalities is the very one you looked at earlier in Figure 53.[1] Here, again, is the constraint polygon: the points within it satisfy all four constraints now trans-

1. We set up this chapter so that you would become familiar with this system of inequalities before we showed you a real-life application.

lated into inequalities.

$$x + y \leq 60 \text{ acres}$$

$$3x + y \leq 90 \text{ gallons}$$

$$x \geq 0$$

$$y \geq 0$$

The algebra problem translated into a geometric problem reads:

Of all the points in the constraint polygon choose the one whose coordinates maximize P in the expression 60x + 50y = P.

If we pick any point in the constraint polygon, read off its coordinates (x,y), and then plug them into our expression $60x + 50y = P$, we can calculate the profit of that particular allocation of acreage to corn and/or soybeans. Note that we don't yet know which points in the constraint polygon will give the *greatest* profit, but we do know that every point within the constraint polygon is realistic in terms of the acreage and herbicide limitations. So, we can trust our constraint polygon to keep us within bounds. Let's choose a few allocations and see how the system works.

Choosing Allocations

What would the profit be if the farmer planted 15 acres with corn and 30 acres with soybeans? That trial solution is represented by point Q (Figure 55) where $x = 15$, $y = 30$. See what happens when we plug these values of x and y into the profit equation $60x + 50y = P$ (in dollars).

$$60(15) + 50(30) = P$$

$$900 + 1,500 = 2,400 \text{ (dollars)}$$

If the farmer planted 15 acres of corn and 30 acres of soybeans, he would make $900 from his corn and $1,500 from his soybeans for a total profit of $2,400. This is not the only way the farmer could make $2,400. The equation $60x + 50y = \$2,400$ can be plotted as a straight line that goes through the point Q. If we draw the line through Q (Figure 56) by letting $x = 0$ and plotting y, then letting

Figure 55

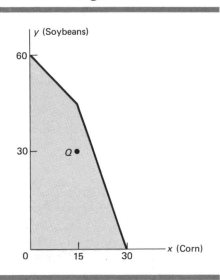

Figure 56

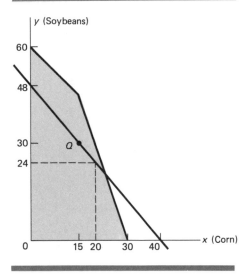

$y = 0$ and plotting x (the usual way), we can find a few more possible allocations that total $2,400. One solution is (20,24), which lies on the line $60x + 50y = 2,400$, meaning that if we plant 20 acres of corn and 24 acres of soybeans we would have a $2,400 profit.

In terms of the farmer's problem, all of the points on the line through Q will produce a profit of $2,400. In other words, there are numerous ways of dividing the farmer's total acreage that satisfy the four constraints and produce a profit of $2,400. Is there another allocation within the bounded polygon that delivers *more* profit?

Maximizing Profit

There was nothing special about our first trial solution of 15 acres of corn and 30 acres of soybeans. Like point Q, this combination was chosen at random. So there is nothing special about the profit value of $2,400. If we choose a different point, R, (Figure 57) inside the polygon, having coordinates $x = 10$, $y = 20$, (10,20) for

Figure 57

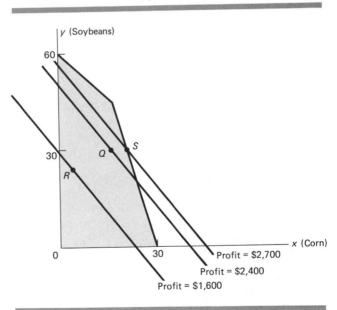

example, and then plug these new x and y values into our profit equation, we would get a profit of

$$60x + 50y = P$$
$$60(10) + 50(20) = P$$
$$600 + 1,000 = 1,600 \quad \text{(in dollars)}.$$

Or, we can choose point S with coordinates $x = 20$, $y = 30$ $(20,30)$ (Figure 57) and find the profit calculation from 20 acres of corn and 30 acres of soybeans to be

$$60x + 50y = P$$
$$60(20) + 50(30) = P$$
$$1,200 + 1,500 = 2,700 \quad \text{(in dollars)}.$$

This is the best profit so far.

The general pattern has become clear. For any point inside the constraint polygon, there is a profit, P, associated with the corresponding planting decision. If the point has coordinates (x,y) then the profit P is given by the equation

$$60x + 50y = P.$$

For each value of P this equation describes a straight line. We have already examined three randomly chosen cases.

$$\text{First trial:} \quad P = \$2,400$$
$$\text{Second trial:} \quad P = \$1,600$$
$$\text{Third trial:} \quad P = \$2,700$$

The equation $60x + 50y = P$, then, seems to describe a *family* of parallel lines (Figure 58), each line corresponding to a different value of P. As we move upward on this ladder of parallels, the profit P increases, so we would like to move upward as far as possible and still remain within the constraint polygon.

Now we have succeeded in reducing the farmer's problem to one of geometry. You can see from the graph in Figure 58 that we

Figure 58

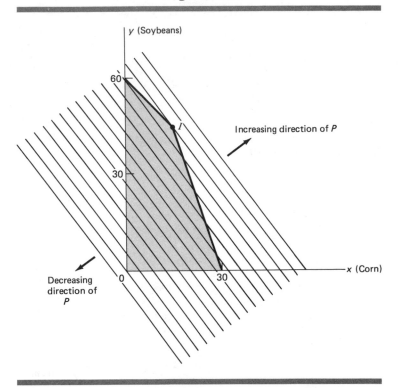

can climb the ladder of parallel lines and stay with the polygon only as far as the point labeled *I*. In linear programming that point *I* is called a *corner point*, or an "extreme point," and it represents the *optimum solution* to the problem because it is the outermost point on the parallel lines that is still within the constraint polygon. (In an algebraic rendering of a more complex linear programming problem, many corner points would be examined in the search for an optimum.) Point *I* has the coordinates $x = 15$, $y = 45$ (15,45) which means the most profitable decision for the farmer would be to plant 15 acres of corn and 45 acres of soybeans for a total profit of $3,150 (Figure 59).

$$60x + 50y = P$$

$$60(15) + 50(45) = P$$

$$900 + 2,250 = 3,150 \quad \text{(in dollars)}$$

Figure 59

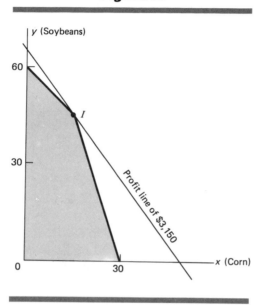

Solving More Complex LP Problems

In solving more complex problems of this nature, linear programmers don't need to plot *all* the parallel lines. Once they get the constraint polygon properly drawn, they take all the corner points shown in Figure 60 (in this example there are just four—*I*, *J*, *K*, and *L*) and try them out in the profit equation. The one that produces the largest profit (in this case point *I*) is then taken to be the optimum.

This "vertex hopping" (each corner point is called a vertex) is the essence of linear programming, even when the number of variables and the number of constraints are too great to be represented on a two- or three-dimensional graph. The algebraic method of solving complex linear-programming problems basically *steers* the computer from vertex to vertex within an imagined geometric figure to find the optimum solution. Thus, most linear-programming problems are solved algebraically in two essential steps:

1. Create a constraint polygon algebraically.
2. Move from vertex to vertex to test for optimization.

Figure 60

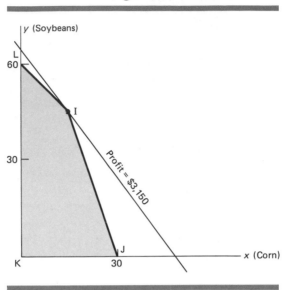

Agriculture, Algebra, and Geometry

The key to success in solving the farmer's problem was the ability to translate the problem from one language into another. We just moved through the three different word-worlds of agriculture, algebra, and geometry. Schematically, what we have been doing can be represented as in Figure 61.

The agricultural problem was not solved directly but in the sequence indicated by the arrows. Most of our energy was not spent solving the problem as it was stated, but in translating it into a form in which it was relatively easy to solve—in this case, a geometric form. This is typical of much mathematical problem solving. We keep going up the ladder of translations until we hit a form of the problem we know how to handle. The more mathematics you know, of course, the more levels there will be that are accessible to you. And, with experience, you will develop intuitions about which translations are likely to be the most fruitful.

Just as an engineer will build a scale model of a structure as an aid in solving its design problems, so too we have built algebraic and geometric models of the agricultural problem. As with engineering, the model was easier to work with than the real thing.

Figure 61

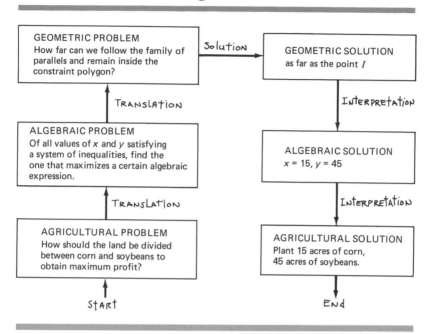

Sensitivity Analysis

Maximum profit may not always be the goal in business. Management might want to maximize distribution, in the case of a new product, or good will. Linear programming is still very useful. The linear-programming model does not set goals. Rather, it forces the planner to express goals and then suggests a series of strategies for meeting them. Such a model can be helpful even when the data are not exact because, when properly used, the model can tell the planner how *sensitive* a particular strategy is to change.

Suppose the profits of $60 per acre of corn and $50 per acre of soybeans were not actual, predictable profits, but only estimates. What would happen to the optimum allocation plan if the actual profits differed significantly from those estimates?

The equation $60x + 50y = P$ described a family of parallel lines. If the numbers 60 and 50 were changed, we would get a *different* family of parallel lines (equations having the same slope

Figure 62

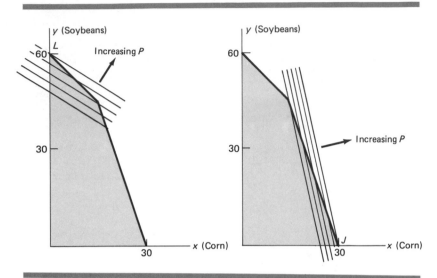

always produce parallel lines when graphed) and possibly a different corner point (*L* or *J* on Figure 62) for our optimum solution.

Or, if the 90-gallon herbicide limit were to be increased to 100 gallons or reduced to 85 gallons, what effect would either of these changes have on the total profit? Since corn requires so much more herbicide per acre than soybeans, it would seem that if the herbicide limit were reduced severely, the corn acreage might have to be reduced to an extent that would make it unprofitable to plant any corn at all. The problem of finding out what that herbicide limit is going to do to the farmer's decision can be solved through linear programming.

Subjecting the model to changes in the given data is called *sensitivity analysis* and is a key component in management and planning both in the private and public sectors today. Congress, for example, routinely asks the U.S. Army Corps of Engineers and the Bureau of Reclamation (the nation's two dam-building agencies) to calculate the sensitivity of the benefits of a proposed dam to changes in, say, the interest rate on construction loans, or the price of electric power to be generated by the dam, or other factors. A manufacturer will want to know how sensitive a proposed new plant is to changes in any of the elements in the cost of construction or in the market for his product.

What often happens with real-life problems is that the long process of solving a problem mathematically results in a solution that generates new questions. This is because mathematics gives planners the power to *test* their theories against all kinds of predictable and unpredictable developments. Without that power, they would have to make decisions based on intuition and common sense, which can't be quantified or tested in advance. Without linear programming, planning would have to be based on what worked in the past rather than what might be possible in the present and future.

Modern-Day LP Problems

In the farmer's problem, there were only two variables, the number of acres of corn to be planted (x) and the number of acres of soybeans (y). Most decision-making problems in business and industry involve hundreds, thousands, or even tens of thousands of variables. With two, we can work within a simple two-dimensional constraint polygon. With three variables we would have to construct a *constraint polyhedron,* a solid in three-dimensional space.

A constraint polyhedron might look like Figure 63. Where we previously climbed a ladder of parallel lines to find our optimum solution to the farmer's problem, we now would have a ladder of

Figure 63

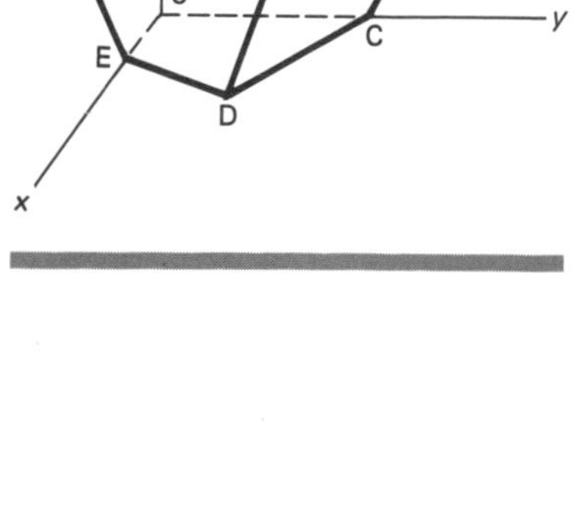

parallel planes (or faces) cutting through the solid. You'll notice that there are nine vertices (corner points) in this three-dimensional constraint polyhedron. If we were solving this problem we would go vertex hopping from point A to point H (including the vertex at zero), each time testing the corner points in the profit equation.

But, if the constraints were still more numerous and the variables still more complex, the constraint polyhedron would have so many faces and vertices that it would be impossible to visualize the problem geometrically.

Figure 64

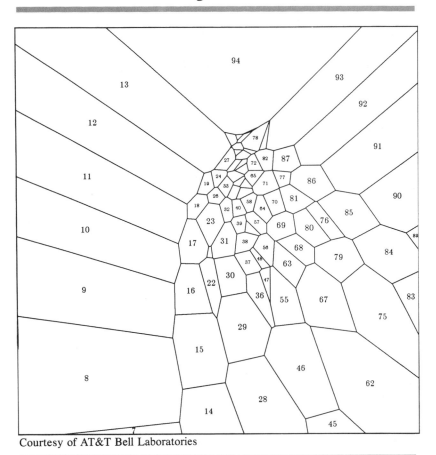

Courtesy of AT&T Bell Laboratories

Yet, the geometry of these problems remains the model for their solution. Figure 64 is the projection of a linear-programming model designed at AT&T's Bell Laboratories to deal with the construction of the Pacific Basin Telecommunications Network, which is intended to link all of the countries (and islands) that border the Pacific Ocean.

There are 94 faces on this particular LP model, which represents only a portion of the problem to be solved. What is interesting about all this, in terms of the insights Descartes originally brought to the study of algebra, is that in advanced linear programming the problem remains expressible in geometric terms even though it can only be solved algebraically. Think of how empowering that combination of geometric insight and algebraic skills can be!

Part

III

From School Mathematics to the Real World

Chapter

7

Social Science: Researching Sex-Role Attitudes

In high school, the field is called social studies because history, civics, government, sociology, economics, psychology, and anthropology all deal with the social aspects of human behavior. You may enjoy these subjects because they explore interesting facts and events and allow for discussion and debate. While there are some numbers among the facts, high school social studies doesn't really require any mathematical skills. At the college level, however, social studies becomes social science: no longer just a body of findings, but a method of inquiry as well. In college you are responsible for knowing not only the conclusions of social research but how to derive and evaluate them as well. To do this, you will have to master social-science research methods that are based largely on the mathematical principles of probability and statistics.

While mathematics is not a subject of social science, it has become one of its most important tools. As a result, statistics and

151

probability are a virtual prerequisite for any major in social, political, or behavioral science. Not surprisingly, college departments of economics, sociology, political science, psychology, and business, as well as mathematics offer courses in statistics and probability. Besides deciding on which of these to take and in what order, you must also decide what level you want to reach. At the least, you will want to learn enough to be able to read research reports in your field and know *about* the tools that the researcher used. On a second, higher level, you may want to be able to do those statistical procedures yourself, in order to analyze data *you* collect. On yet a third level, you may want to know how to derive such procedures from mathematical principles, in which case you would need a course in mathematical statistics. And, finally, should you want to tackle some new problems in analysis, you would need to know about operations research, computer science, and stochastic processes. In any event, you won't be able to go very far in the study of social behavior without some familiarity with statistics and probability.

The Importance of Measuring

The work of social science, much like the work of a detective, involves detailed observations. But to make sense of what they see, social scientists also have to develop ways to *measure* their findings in order to be able to compare them, and to develop theories—hypotheses and models—to *explain* them. The point of social science—any science—is to be able to generalize about other, as yet unexamined, situations. So, in addition to good detective skills like patience and careful observation, the social scientist needs to cultivate imagination to go beyond the obvious. Sherlock Holmes is always telling Dr. Watson that his conclusions are "elementary," but they are only obvious to Holmes because he has some theory on which to hang them. Still, neither the detective's nor the social researcher's theories are worth much if they do not stand up to the evidence provided by the real world.

The subject of social research is both quite old and new, human beings having been interested in themselves and in one another since the beginning of time. Royal chroniclers recorded the high points of their sovereigns' reigns. Royal demographers took population counts, and explorers like Marco Polo made copious notes about distant places and interpreted them for their countrymen at home. All of this was social research, though it might not have been called that at the time.

The more systematic study of humans as social beings is a recent development. Beginning in the nineteenth century, these studies increasingly tended to involve mathematics. Numbers, quite simply, made the human parade much more meaningful. Today, psychology, sociology, anthropology, political science, economics, and even history have become dependent upon the techniques of sampling, mathematical modeling, statistical testing, and probability—in short, upon mathematical manipulations.

As you will see, the raw material of social science remains its data: collectible information about people's attitudes, behaviors, responses, and interactions. But data collection is only the *beginning* of social researchers' work. And, unlike their predecessors, today's social-science students need to master new tools involving mathematics in order to pursue the study of humankind.

Dr. MacCorquodale's Research Project

Dr. Patricia MacCorquodale is a sociologist at the University of Arizona in Tucson who specializes in the way sex roles and sex role expectations are changing in different population groups. She is interested not only in how young men and women perceive themselves in grown-up roles in *general*; she also wants to know whether the perceptions of white teenagers, or "Anglos" as they are called in the American Southwest, differ from those of Mexican-American young people. In the particular project described below, she wanted to compare the attitudes toward work and family of young men and women of the Anglo and Hispanic populations in southern Arizona.

Like all researchers, Dr. MacCorquodale began her project with a "literature search"—a look at all of the previous studies that had been done on sex roles and attitudes toward work and family. She did this to be certain she was not repeating the work of another social researcher and to find an appropriate research tool—a method that would lead her to new conclusions. She knew that she couldn't survey everyone in the Southwest, so she had to select a target population for her study. She also knew that some people don't answer questionnaires honestly or completely, so she studied other researchers' "instruments," as questionnaires are called, to find out what works and what doesn't.

Her search of previous work showed that while the changing roles of white women in America have been well documented, there is little information about the Mexican-American family. So, if Dr. MacCorquodale could locate willing subjects among Mexican-American young people and compare them to subjects within the Anglo community, she could make a significant contribution to her field.

Her search also revealed some interesting trends in the American population as a whole. In middle-class white families, changing sex roles have accompanied changing work roles for women. As more and more women have entered the labor force, their expectations of themselves, their families, and their futures have changed correspondingly. She knew from other studies that Mexican-American women have been much less likely to have jobs than Anglo women. One question, then, is whether young Mexican-American women, who have grown up with their mothers at home, would be more "traditional" or "nontraditional" (two attitudes Dr. MacCorquodale was going to try to define more precisely and measure) in their attitudes and expectations than Anglo women.

She also knew from previous work in the field that Anglo males, even in the 1980s, have more traditional notions of "appropriate" sex roles for females than white females have for themselves. Would this difference in the way males and females view the roles of women hold true for Mexican-American males and females too?

These reflections led Dr. MacCorquodale to a more precise formulation of her research question. Instead of just a broad general inquiry into young women's sex-role expectations across two different ethnic groups, she was able to devise four very specific hypotheses to test within a scientific framework. These hypotheses interested her, not only because they were as yet unexplored, but also, and more important, because they could be tested.

Sampling

In sociology, as in all other sciences, the investigator is seeking some kind of truth. An experiment must be replicable; that is, when it is done a second, a tenth, or even a millionth time by other researchers, the results should be more or less the same. A survey such as Dr. MacCorquodale's must produce results that are true in general, not just for those particular people interviewed. At the completion of her research, Dr. MacCorquodale wanted to be able to make an accurate statement about all or most Mexican-American and Anglo girls and boys, even though she could not possibly survey *all* of the young people between the ages of 11 and 16 who are white or Mexican American.

Her first chore, then, was to select a *sample* of subjects (a portion of a larger group) in such a way that they were *representative* of all. Her subjects had to be selected at random like the numbers in a lottery so that there was no bias in the choice. For example, if *only* daughters of working mothers were questioned, we could not accept her results as an accurate representation of the views of all or most Mexican-American or Anglo girls, because we know *all* mothers do not work. By the same argument, if *none* of her subjects had working mothers, we would be comparably skeptical of her findings. This type of selection error, which researchers call "sampling bias," produces an inaccurate conclusion. For instance, if you wanted to test the hypothesis that the favorite sport of all teenagers is basketball, but interviewed only boys over six feet tall, your data would all have come from the type of person most likely to play basketball and would be skewed.

Representative Sampling

The words "sample," "representative," and "bias" refer to issues in sociology that mathematics can help illuminate. Dr.

MacCorquodale's research problem was nonmathematical; it was qualitative rather than quantitative since it dealt with attitudes and expectations. Still, Dr. MacCorquodale could not have begun her work without employing some of the mathematical principles of probability and statistics.

Her sample—the students to whom questionnaires were given—was made up of students from two areas in southern Arizona. A questionnaire was given to 304 junior high school students and 607 senior high school students from a town on the Mexican border and the same questionnaire was administered to 535 junior high school students and 997 senior high school students from four schools located in a medium-sized city elsewhere in Arizona. The border-town school is 80 percent Mexican-American; the city system, only 20 percent. Thus, she had a considerable difference in ethnic identity in her two locations.[1]

Let's look more closely at the makeup of her sample. From a total of 2,443 students she decided to remove those who were neither Anglo nor Mexican American, leaving 2,065 subjects to be investigated and compared along gender and ethnic lines. While her sample included many more Mexican-American than Anglo teenagers, there were about the same number of males and females in each ethnic group.

Males		Females	
Anglos	Mexican Americans	Anglos	Mexican Americans
239	755	237	834

One of the advantages of regional studies is that the researcher can look closely at a particular ethnic or racial minority. In the U.S. population as a whole, it would be difficult to find a way to "over-sample," as this technique is called, an ethnic minority. But in

---

1. No sample is perfect. For example, dropouts could not be interviewed. If they were a sizable part of the school populations and if their attitudes were considerably different, her results could be a little skewed. Social science research always has to contend with such possibilities and Dr. MacCorquodale is well aware of them.

southern Arizona, there are many Mexican-American communities from which to choose.

Ninety-seven percent of her subjects returned their questionnaires. This is a high response rate and is very important in eliminating bias. If a large percentage of students had not filled out the questionnaire, the possible reason for this low response rate would have clouded the issues Dr. MacCorquodale wanted to study: Were the boys, more than the girls, troubled by the questions or unwilling to answer them? With only 3 percent not participating, Dr. MacCorquodale could be reasonably certain that virtually *all* of her subjects were willing and able to participate.

But we are still left with a key question in social-science research. What made her sample representative? Why sould we believe that her findings will be true for all or most Anglo and Mexican-American young people? This is where mathematics comes in as an essential tool.

Random Number Sampling

A researcher who needs an unbiased selection method will go to a *random number table*, usually found in the back of any standard statistics textbook, to find a numerical sequence that does not follow a pattern. Obviously 1, 2, 3, 4, 5 . . . is not random; neither is 2, 4, 6, 8. . . . The sequence 7, 9, 14, 18, 21, 27 . . . isn't random either. This pattern is based on multiplications involving two integers (7 and 9), as you can see below:

$$\underbrace{(2 \times 7)}_{14}, \underbrace{(2 \times 9)}_{18}, \underbrace{(3 \times 7)}_{21}, \underbrace{(3 \times 9)}_{27} \text{ and so on.}$$

Before there were computers, selecting random numbers involved spinning dials and noting the numbers as they showed up. Today, computers are used to generate random number tables because they can do tedious arithmetic very quickly. You could program a computer to do a series of numerical manipulations and then use the resulting digits as your random numbers. The following sequence comes from a scientific calculator with a built-in program that generates random numbers between zero and one. All we had to do was press "random" to get each of the following three-digit numbers.

.531	.490
.574	.751
.072	.436
.924	.099

At first look, these may not seem random enough. There are two numbers in the .500 group, two in the .400 group, and two in the .000 group. However, in this case each three-digit decimal number between 0 and 1 had an equally likely chance of occurring. That's what makes this a random number table. Random numbers can cluster. They just don't follow *predictable* or *recurring* patterns.

This may seem like a lot of trouble to go to just to get rid of any numerical patterns or sequences. But the normal human mind can't help thinking in patterns. Try to come up with some three-digit random numbers yourself. After about 10, or maybe 20 tries if you exert great discipline, your numbers will begin to show some kind of repeating pattern. Even if you make an effort *not* to repeat any numbers, or to have doubles or any other familiar numerical sequence, the very fact that you are trying *not* to repeat will skew the randomness of the process. Randomness means the absence of any pattern or purpose, and that, for our human brains, is a very difficult thing to achieve.

Applying Random Numbers

When it came to interviewing students in the several schools she had chosen for her research, Dr. MacCorquodale did not need to do a random selection. She simply administered her questionnaire to all seventh-grade math students and all tenth-grade English students. (English and math are required subjects, so she had access to all of the students through these classes.) But, in addition to the students, Dr. MacCorquodale also wanted to get some background information from their parents. Out of 2,065 sets of parents she wanted to question only 250. In order to select 250 sets of parents from 2,065 without skewing her data she used random sampling.

Let's look again at the list of random numbers between zero and one that were generated by a scientific calculator.

.531	.490
.574	.751
.072	.436
.924	.099

If Dr. MacCorquodale multiplied each of these random numbers by the total number of parent-pairs in the group—2,065—she would get some random products to use in selecting the parents to interview. Let's try a few. Take the random number, multiply it by the total number of parents in the group, and then select the couple in that position on the list.

Random Number	Total No. of Parents	Parent-Pair to be Interviewed
.531 ×	2,065	= 1,097th couple on the list
.574 ×	2,065	= 1,185th couple on the list
.072 ×	2,065	= 149th couple on the list
.924 ×	2,065	= 1,908th couple on the list
.099 ×	2,065	= 204th couple on the list

If she continued to generate random numbers until she had 250 of them and continued to multiply each number by the total number of parents, she would have a truly randomly generated selection of parents to interview. If the system were truly random (you might have already noticed) some sets of parents might have come up twice. In that case the researcher would have had to interview them twice or simply score them twice in order to keep out sample bias.

Because the random numbers fall between 0 and 1, the result of multiplying any one of them by 2,065 will be between 0 and 2,065. That's why generating very small random numbers, that is, numbers between 0 and 1, is useful in getting numbers or positions that fall within the limits of your target population.

In reporting her research, Dr. MacCorquodale did not have to describe in any detail how she made her random selection. By simply stating that the 250 sets of parents interviewed were randomly selected, people familiar with statistical sampling knew that she used random number procedures to choose them from the larger group.

Stratified Samples

Sampling methods will vary with the research subject. Most of the time it is not feasible (or desirable) to poll or interview everyone in the population under study. The Nielsen ratings, which measure the popularity of TV programs, are based on the viewing choices of about 1,400 households. Nielsen researchers monitor those 1,400 TV sets to predict, by means of generalization (called *extrapolation* in statistical jargon), what *millions* of households are watching. What makes the Nielsen results believable? We can accept the fact that 1,400 households are representative of 100 million because sampling procedures are used in such a way as to achieve both randomness within certain population groups and coverage of the many different kinds of people who watch TV.

Another example of sampling meant to reflect the views of *all* Americans is in a newspaper story based on a national poll taken to determine Americans' views of apartheid in South Africa. Only 1,462 people were polled for this article, but the headline reads: "Americans [not *some* Americans or *certain* Americans] are unsure of solution in South Africa."

You are probably thinking that no random selection of so few could possibly be representative, and, indeed, you are right. However, such pollsters do not randomly select people from all of the telephone listings in the country. Instead, they create a kind of sociopolitical map of the nation's citizens and randomly select from various categories such as blacks, whites, Hispanics, veterans, nonveterans, women, men, urban, rural, big city, small city, working class, middle class, upper-middle class, farmers, Democrats, Republicans, Independents, college educated, not college educated, and so on.

Collecting opinions in this way is called *stratified random sampling* because not everyone in the population has an equal chance to be chosen. The intention behind such stratified random sampling is to ensure that every important identifiable group in the country is represented. In fact, in many of these national samples, minority groups are oversampled. Typically, pollsters would do the kind of categorization seen in Table 18 when selecting a group of 1,500.

Table 18

Whites	Blacks	Native Americans	Hispanics	Asian Americans
300	300	300	300	300
(65%)	(2%)	(8%)	(20%)	(5%)

(The actual proportions of these population groups in Arizona are given in parentheses.)

Then, they would randomly select from the population, screening for ethnicity and race. When they reached 300 whites (which would happen fairly quickly), they would stop. When they reached 300 Hispanics, they would stop sampling that group, and so on, until they had polled 300 of each group. Polls frequently oversample minority or specialized groups in order to compare, for example, black voters to white ones, Jewish foreign-policy attitudes to those of Catholics, consumers to farmers, and so forth. But, to get any kind of *overall* picture for Arizona, one would then have to *weight* the responses; that is, multiply the data collected by the proportion. Thus, if 55 percent of the whites polled said "yes" on a questionnaire and 70 percent of the blacks, 40 percent of the Hispanics, 20 percent of the Asian Americans, and 20 percent of the Native Americans said "yes," the total percentage of the sample responding "yes" would be the sum of the following products, or 48 percent.

.55 × .65 (fraction of whites in the population)	= .358
.70 × .02 (fraction of blacks in the population)	= .014
.40 × .20 (fraction of Hispanics in the population)	= .080
.20 × .05 (fraction of Asian Americans in the population)	= .010
.20 × .08 (fraction of Native Americans in the population)	= .016
Total	= .478

Error Margins

One of the most embarrassing polling errors ever made occurred during the hotly contested Truman–Dewey race for the presidency in 1948. The race was close and immediately before the election the pollsters were finding Governor Dewey, the Republican candidate, ahead. Forced to select their headlines for the next day before all of the election results were in (before computers and communication satellites, newspaper deadlines were significantly earlier than now), newspaper editors went with Dewey: "Dewey Beats Truman." "Dewey Wins." "Dewey, the Next President." The only trouble was that Truman won and when the poll data were reviewed, it turned out that an *error margin*—the plus or minus of a few percentage points—had skewed the predictions just enough to signal the wrong winner. Ever since that event, responsible pollsters and researchers have tried to make a quantitative assessment of the reliability of their results because even with the most carefully executed sampling there are small but sometimes crucial margins of error.

These statements of error margin sometimes appear at the very end of a published report in a newspaper or magazine, so you have to look carefully for them. But they are worth examining if you are going to assess properly the meaning and significance of a survey. Error margin will usually be given in terms of the percentage points of *variance* as in the following example:

> *If one could have questioned all Americans with telephones, there is only 1 chance in 20 that the findings would vary more than 3 percentage points either way.*

This error margin is very important in reporting statistical information based on samples smaller than the entire population. We know that not everyone was or could have been polled. We assume that the pollsters were careful in selecting their sample and in tallying the responses to the questions asked. Statistical procedures enable them to have a certain confidence in their results. To reassure us, the public, that their findings are true, they give us the *error margin*—in this case, plus or minus 3 percentage points—and also their *level of confidence*, which in this case is that there is only a 1 in 20 chance that their error margin is greater than this.

This is important in understanding results of that poll where blacks were found to be more concerned than whites with South Africa's fate. According to the report, "Half of the blacks polled thought U.S. business should get out of South Africa, and only 31 percent of the whites thought we should." This is a significant difference.

How confident can we be that this difference would show up if *all* American blacks and whites were polled? The error margin and the confidence level give us the answer: There is only a 1 in 20 (5

Figure 65

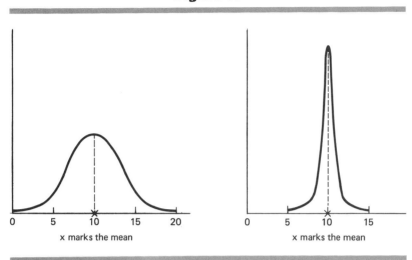

x marks the mean   x marks the mean

percent) chance that these percentages are off by more than 3 percent either way. That is, "half of the blacks" can be no more than 53 percent and no less then 47 percent. Thirty-one percent of the whites can be no more than 34 percent, no less than 28 percent. This statement of the *variance* possible gives us more confidence in the generalization. Let's see why variance is so important.

Variation Around the Mean

We make use of averages all the time. We talk of average height, average income, average scores on a particular standardized test. The technical term for average is *mean,* and to calculate means you add up the wages or heights or scores of everybody in the group you are surveying and divide those sums by the number of people in the group.

There is no question that averages are useful, but it is important to distinguish between averages that result from wide and narrow variation. We need a way to describe the range of variation and then to interpret, depending on the research subject, how important that range is to our results.

The two drawings in Figure 65 represent a common curve in statistics called the *normal distribution.* Notice that while both curves represent distributions having the same mean or average, the degree of variation in the one is quite wide, ranging from about 5 to 15 units, and the degree of variation in the other is narrow, ranging from about 9 to 11 units. You can see that, whenever you are given a mean, it is very useful to know the *degree of variation* involved. Although the means in the two drawings are the same (10), the spread of the points (the distributions) are very different. On the right, where there is little variation, the mean is a fairly good description of the group—things, people, quantities. The large variation on the left tells us that the average does not adequately reflect the variation within the group.

Generating and Testing Hypotheses

Dr. MacCorquodale was going to be very careful when interpreting her data, the answers to the questionnaires she administered. She had derived some specific hypotheses from her literature search, and with the help of statistical procedures she planned to test these ideas to make certain she was not reading too much into what she had collected.

From her general curiosity about how young Anglo and Mexican-American males and females see their future roles, Dr. MacCorquodale developed four specific hypotheses to test:

Hypothesis 1: Mexican Americans (of both sexes) hold more traditional attitudes toward sex roles than Anglos.

Hypothesis 2: This difference also holds true in their attitudes toward sex roles in the family and at work.

Hypothesis 3: Males of both ethnic groups hold more traditional sex-role beliefs than females.

Hypothesis 4: Mexican-American males have more traditional sex-role beliefs than Anglo males.

To test these hypotheses, Dr. MacCorquodale, like any experienced survey researcher, designed her questionnaire in such a way that it did not draw attention to the actual subject of her research.

She spread the sex-role items among a long series of questions about students' educational and work goals, attitudes toward various school subjects, how they think they are doing in school in general, and other background topics. The 24 sex-role questions were coded, however, in such a way that Dr. MacCorquodale could analyze them separately. Using each student's answers to these key questions, and knowing whether the respondent was male or female, Anglo or Mexican-American, Dr. MacCorquodale could begin to try to figure out how her subjects viewed sex roles by their ethnicity, by gender, and by gender and ethnicity combined.

Data Analysis

Let's take just one of her sex-role-related questions and see how she analyzed it.

Item: Women should be able to compete with men for jobs, such as telephone linesman, that have usually belonged to men. Choose one of the following five responses:

1. Strongly agree
2. Agree
3. Disagree
4. Strongly disagree
5. No answer; don't know

Dr. MacCorquodale's first task was to tabulate the answers to this item by group, first by Anglo males (Table 19). Next, she computed the *percentages* of these Anglo males' responses (Table 20).

Table 19

	Anglo Males
Strongly agree	53
Agree	137
Disagree	27
Strongly disagree	18
No answer; don't know	4
Total	239

She then proceeded to do the same calculations with the three other groups: Anglo females, Mexican-American males, and Mexican-American females. Out of these computations came the results shown in Table 21. The results of this question seem to support Dr. MacCorquodale's thinking. The responses "disagree" and "strongly disagree" are interpreted to mean that the respondents have traditional views of sex differences, and, indeed, the males of both ethnic groups seem to be more traditional. Furthermore, Mexican-American males seem to be the most traditional of all: 28.4 percent of them (21.3 percent + 7.1 percent) disagree and strongly disagree with the statement, compared with 18.8 percent of the Anglo males, 9.3 percent of the Anglo females, and 17.4 percent of the Mexican-American females.

Table 20

	Anglo Males	
	Number who chose this answer	Percentage who chose this answer
Strongly agree	53	22.2%
Agree	137	57.3
Disagree	27	11.3
Strongly disagree	18	7.5
No answer; don't know	4	1.7
Total	239	100.0%

This kind of computation had to be done on *all* 24 sex-role-related questions before Dr. MacCorquodale could draw any major conclusions. But, even if the other 23 sets of answers showed the same pattern, we would need to be convinced that these responses reflected beliefs and values that could be generalized to more than 2,065 southern Arizonans. We would want to know whether the differences in the distributions of responses were due to *chance* or to real differences in attitudes between boys and girls, Anglos and Mexican Americans. Finding the likelihood as to whether these answers could have happened by chance brings us to some of the most important mathematical techniques in social science research,

Table 21

	Males		Females	
	Anglos	Mexican Americans	Anglos	Mexican Americans
Strongly agree	53 (22.2)	147 (19.5)	114 (48.1)	256 (30.7)
Agree	137 (57.3)	387 (51.3)	98 (41.3)	427 (51.2)
Disagree	27 (11.3)	161 (21.3)	17 (7.2)	112 (13.4)
Strongly disagree	18 (7.5)	54 (7.1)	5 (2.1)	33 (4.0)
No answer; don't know	4 (1.7)	6 (.8)	3 (1.3)	6 (.7)
Total	239 (100)	755 (100)	237 (100)	834 (100)

Percentages are shown in parentheses.

techniques without which social science couldn't be a science at all. Dr. MacCorquodale is going to have to *prove* that the results of her survey *could not have occurred by chance.*

The Null Hypothesis and Chi-Square

One procedure social science researchers use to find the probability that their results could have happened by chance is known as *testing the null hypothesis.* The null hypothesis is simply the reverse of the researcher's hypothesis. For example, Dr. MacCorquodale's starting point is that the variation in the answers to her questions about sex roles reflects differences in attitudes among Anglo and Mexican-American males and females. The opposite or null hypothesis would be that the differences in the answers reflect only chance variation or accident—nothing special at all.

In social research, it is very difficult to prove positive hypotheses beyond the shadow of a doubt. Attitudes and beliefs are hard to measure despite the best-written questionnaires. The researcher is never entirely sure whether two people read the same meaning into the same statement or whether the one who answered "strongly disagree" on the question about jobs for women might have answered differently the next day. But it is not so hard to prove or disprove the null hypothesis, thanks to some mathematical techniques that are based on probability and statistics.

You may wonder how anyone can *prove* that results were not haphazard. Fortunately, social science researchers can apply a procedure called the chi-square test (pronounced "ki square") or goodness-of-fit test. By the time you complete this chapter, you will understand chi-square (written mathematically using the Greek chi—χ^2), know why it's important, and even be able to do the analysis yourself!

Significant Differences

The chi-square test is a way of checking the null hypothesis—that there are *no* significant differences among the answers. Applying the null hypothesis to Dr. MacCorquodale's question about women competing with men for jobs, a group of Anglo male teenagers who had no particular bias in their attitude would have responded like this:

Strongly agree	20%
Agree	20%
Disagree	20%
Strongly disagree	20%
No answer; don't know	20%

In other words, if nothing really influenced them, their responses might have been distributed about evenly over the five answer categories. Looking at Table 22, we can see immediately that the answers Dr. MacCorquodale recorded on this question were not 20 percent across the board. The actual or *observed* response to "strongly agree" is pretty close to chance (22.2 percent as against 20 percent) and the response to "disagree" is not too far off. But the actual "agree," "strongly disagree," and "no answer" responses are nowhere near the 20 percent *expected* response rate. By simply looking at these comparisons, Dr. MacCorquodale could begin to be somewhat confident that the answers reflected real differences. But suppose she wanted to be sure that there was only a 1 in 50 probability (or a 2 percent chance) that these results could

Table 22

	Anglo Males' Actual (observed) Response (%)	Null-Hypothesis (expected) Response (%)
Strongly agree	22.2	20
Agree	57.3	20
Disagree	11.3	20
Strongly disagree	7.5	20
No answer; don't know	1.7	20

have occurred by chance. How could she translate her desired confidence level into a disproof of the null hypothesis?

This is where the chi-square test was useful. To do a chi-square test of her data, she created another table showing the actual outcomes by percentage for each question and each group ("observed," or O) compared to the chance outcomes by percentage for each question and each group ("expected," or E). Let's follow a complete chi-square analysis for the question we've been looking at, considering only the answer distribution of the Anglo males. In Table 23, the percentages have been rounded for the sake of simplicity.

The fact that some of the differences between observed (O) and expected (E) responses are positive and others are negative doesn't matter in this kind of analysis because the researcher is looking for the *amount of difference,* not whether it is positive or negative. The

Table 23. Chi-Square Analysis of Anglo Males' Responses to Question 1

	O (percentage)	E (percentage)	O minus E (percentage difference)
Strongly agree	22	20	+2
Agree	57	20	+37
Disagree	11	20	−9
Strongly disagree	8	20	−12
No answer; don't know	2	20	−18

signs disappear when the differences are squared anyway. Whether 9 is positive ($+9$) or negative (-9), its square is 81. Some of the actual responses will be higher than the expected; some lower. The important thing is the degree of difference.

The formula for calculating the chi-square number that tells the researcher how *sure* she can be that the results could not have happened by chance looks rather formidable at first. But once you start to plug in numbers, you will see that the computations involve only arithmetic and simple algebra. It is not a conceptually difficult tool to use but if your calculator is not programmed to do chi-square, it is fairly tedious.

Here is the formula written in mathematical symbols (Σ indicates that a sequence of values will be summed).

$$\chi^2 = \sum_{i=1}^{k} \frac{(O_i - E_i)^2}{E_i}$$

(k is a constant, the number of total responses possible.) This is described in words as follows:

The chi-square number equals the sum of the squares of all the differences between the observed (O) and the expected (E) outcomes, divided by the expected (E) in each case.

You don't have to know how this formula is derived mathematically, and it is not important that you memorize it right away. Professionals don't memorize all formulas. They generally work with tables of statistics and statistical reference books close at hand. The sign of a professional in any field is knowing where to go for information when it is needed.

Let's look at the chi-square equation more closely (k becomes 5 as we plug in a real problem where there are 5 response categories):

$$\chi^2 = \sum_{i=1}^{5} \frac{(O_i - E_i)^2}{E_i}.$$

The Greek letter Σ is sigma which stands for "sum of" and indicates that a series of algebraic expressions will be added together. The $i = 1$ subscript and the 5 above the Σ indicate that all of the ratios are to be summed to solve this equation.

Now we can turn to the calculator to square each difference (O minus E) and divide by the expected (E) (Table 24). Dr. Mac-Corquodale's chi-square in this case was 96.1. She then turned to

Table 24

	O	E	O − E (difference + or −)	$(O - E)^2/20$ (difference squared divided by expected)
Strongly agree	22	20	+ 2	4/20 = .20
Agree	57	20	+37	1369/20 = 68.45
Disagree	11	20	− 9	81/20 = 4.05
Strongly disagree	8	20	− 12	144/20 = 7.2
No answer; don't know	2	20	− 18	324/20 = 16.2
				$\chi^2 = 96.1$

a chi-square table to see whether this particular distribution of answers among the Anglo males could have occurred by chance.

Table 25 is an abbreviated chi-square table, which is found in all statistics textbooks.

Table 25. Chi-Square Table

df	$p = 0.20$	$p = 0.10$	$p = 0.05$	$p = 0.02$	$p = 0.01$
3	4.642	6.251	7.815	9.837	11.341
4	5.989	7.779	9.488	11.668	**13.272**
5	7.289	9.236	11.070	13.388	15.086

The *df* (degrees of freedom) is the result of another calculation, based on one fewer than the total number of response categories. That number determines the *row* of the chi-square table the researcher has to consult. The *p* designates probability in decimals ($p = 0.20$ means there is a 20 percent chance, or 1 in 5, that the result could have occurred by chance).

Dr. MacCorquodale's chi square of 96.1 is well above the number in this portion of the table. Hence, the probability that the distribution of Anglo males' answers to Question 1 could have happened by chance alone is very small; the null hypothesis is not accepted.

Discovering Differences

By means of the first set of chi-square analyses, Dr. Mac-Corquodale was able to prove that her data were meaningful, at least for Anglo male responses to sex-role Question 1. She then had to do the same kind of statistical check on all four groups' responses—*observed* versus *expected*—and on all 24 sets of questions. Once this was done, she could finally turn to what really interested her in those 24 sets of responses and the overall reason for her research study. Remember that she initially wanted to find out whether there were different attitudes toward sex roles among Mexican-American and Anglo young people and, even more important, whether these differences in attitude *corresponded* to their background and gender. To measure and evaluate these differences, she had to compare responses and calculate additional chi-squares.

The first step in discovering differences was to compare responses by ethnicity and gender. Table 26 shows just one such comparison: the observed responses on Question 1 by Anglo and

Table 26. Observed Responses (O's)

	Anglo Males	Mexican-American Males
Strongly agree	53	147
Agree	137	387
Disagree	27	161
Strongly disagree	18	54
Total	235	749

Mexican-American males. (At this stage in the analysis, the "no" and "don't know" answers were eliminated.)

Next she needed to compare these *observed* (that is, actual) differences between the Anglo and the Mexican-American males' responses to some kind of *expected* responses, given their proportions in the population. But this time there were no easy E's to list (like 20 percent across all responses). Rather, she was going to have to generate the E's in all the tables before she could do a chi-square analysis of the gender and ethnic differences in the responses. We will not go through her computations of E's. They involved a lot of tedious arithmetic, but they are based on the same null-hypothesis logic: If ethnicity and gender were *not* important factors, what might the *expected* responses of Anglo and Mexican-American males and females have been? Then if the *observed* responses were signficantly different from those that were *expected,* it would mean it is highly likely that gender and ethnicity *did* make a difference.

Let us skip ahead now to Dr. MacCorquodale's final tables of O's and E's for Anglo and Mexican-American males' responses to sex-role Question 1 and see how, based on the O's and E's for this question, she was able to compute her new chi-squares and test the null-hypothesis each time (Tables 27 and 28).

Adding the two chi-square calculations (8.872 + 2.784) she got a combined chi-square of 11.656.

Table 27

	Anglo Males			
	O	E	O − E	$\frac{O-E}{E}$
Strongly agree	53	47.76	+ 5.24	.575
Agree	137	125.14	+11.86	1.124
Disagree	27	44.90	− 17.90	7.136
Strongly disagree	18	17.20	+ 0.80	0.037
				$\chi^2 = 8.872$

Table 28

	Mexican-American Males			
	O	E	O − E	$\frac{O-E}{E}$
Strongly agree	147	152.24	− 5.24	0.180
Agree	387	398.86	−11.86	0.353
Disagree	161	143.10	+17.90	2.239
Strongly disagree	54	54.80	− .80	0.012
				$\chi^2 = 2.784$

Now, as before, Dr. MacCorquodale went to a chi-square table (Table 29) to check the significance of these differences. As you can see from this abbreviated chi-square table, with a *df* of 3, the chi-square calculation of 11.656 falls at the 0.01 level of significance. That means Dr. MacCorquodale could say with 0.01 probability (1 chance in 100) that the *differences* between Anglo and Mexican-American males' responses to sex-role Question 1 could not have occurred by chance. Hence, the positive hypothesis—that Anglo and Mexican-American males *do* differ in their attitudes toward women working at "men's jobs"—had been established with a high level of confidence.

Table 29

df	$p = 0.20$	$p = 0.10$	$p = 0.05$	$p = 0.02$	$p = 0.01$
3	4.642	6.251	7.815	9.837	**11.341**
4	5.989	7.779	9.488	11.668	13.272
5	7.289	9.236	11.070	13.388	15.086

This was about one quarter of the work Dr. MacCorquodale had to do to test the null hypothesis on that single question about work roles; and she had 23 more questions to analyze using the same procedures. Fortunately, we have all her chi-squares before us and do not have to do them ourselves. Table 30 shows her results on the question we have been examining.

Table 30. Results on Sex-Role Question 1.

Comparison of Anglos to Mexican Americans	
Males $\chi^2 = 11.989$ $\quad p = .01$	**Females** $\chi^2 = 27.68$ $\quad p = .001$
Comparison of Males to Females	
Anglos $\chi^2 = 38.37$ $\quad p = .001$	**Mexican Americans** $\chi^2 = 41.46$ $\quad p = .001$

Table 30, incidentally, is given in the form in which chi-square results would be presented in a professional paper.

The Power of Chi-Square

You now have some idea of how important chi-square is as a research tool. It helps social researchers avoid misinterpreting their data. It also allows them to cross-check to see whether differences in responses are statistically significant or whether there is a reasonable probability that those differences could have occurred by chance alone. Researchers need to do these mathematical tests before they draw conclusions from their surveys lest they accept results that could have been accidental or coincidental.

Research Results

After using a series of chi-square tests to confirm that her results could not have happened by chance, Dr. MacCorquodale concluded that *both* ethnic background and gender are statistically significant variables in predicting different responses to sex-role questions. She documented her conclusions in a table of comparisons of Anglos and Mexican-American males and females (Table 31) showing the chi-square number for each response and the *p* value (the probability that this result could have occurred by chance).

Table 31. Comparisons of Anglos to Mexican Americans

Males	Females
$\chi^2 = 11.656$ $p = .01$	$\chi^2 = 27.68$ $p = .001$
There is 1 chance in 100 that these answers occurred by chance.	There is 1 chance in 1,000 that these answers occurred by chance.
Anglos	**Mexican Americans**
$\chi^2 = 38.37$ $p = .001$	$\chi^2 = 41.46$ $p = .001$
There is 1 chance in 1,000 that these answers occurred by chance.	There is 1 chance in 1,000 that these answers occurred by chance.

Whatever you may feel intuitively about Dr. MacCorquodale's results, you have to accept them as having been systematically tested. Although she used a relatively small sample of the entire Anglo and Mexican-American teenage populations of Arizona, she demonstrated through her sampling techniques and by use of statistical procedures that her choice of subjects did not distort the actual population, and that in this case her response patterns could not have happened by coincidence. This means that even if her questionnaire were given many more times to other Anglo and Mexican-American young people, it is unlikely that the additional data would contradict her findings. Her methodology, her use of statistical inference in a systematic and entirely unbiased way, enabled her to conduct a study that she would never have been able to complete had she been forced to interview the entire population. Her methodology is not just her tool, it is her power.

Statistics, Probability, and You

What we have done in this chapter, looking closely at one piece of social research, is very much like what every scientist does when trying to assess the value of a research experiment. The measurements involved in any scientific experiment are a *sample* of the unlimited set of measurements that would result if the scientist could perform that experiment over and over again, indefinitely. Since no researcher has the means or the time to do an infinite number of repetitions, he or she has to draw inferences as cautiously as possible, testing every null hypothesis along the way. This is why the techniques of chi-square and other kinds of statistical testing are so important today.

If you are going to take a college calculus course (and it is wise to do that as early as possible), try to schedule it before you study statistics. If you take a course in statistics and probability first, many of the concepts and much of the notation will seem forbidding. Once you know calculus, however, all of this will be comfortably familiar. In calculus, you will learn about slopes of lines, measuring and naming curves, minimizing and maximizing functions, calculating areas under a curve, limits, summing series, and many of the techniques that you will use in statistics.

A good solid grounding in statistics and probability opens up career and personal options that would otherwise remain closed. Best of all, these disciplines lend precision to your thinking and give you a powerful tool to use in your course work in college and throughout your professional life.

Chapter

8

Biology: Exploring Population Genetics

Mathematizing Biology

Biology used to be the one science that was comfortably free of mathematics. But during the past 35 years, college-level biology has probably changed more than any other basic science in the breadth and depth of its offerings and, above all, in its reliance on mathematics. In this chapter, we will explore how the biological sciences have become more quantitative and, taking a close look at the research project of a graduate student in microbiology, see how mathematical techniques are being applied today to biological research.

Earlier, biologists (or naturalists, as they used to be called) could avoid mathematics because biology was not the experimental science it has since become. Biologists did not formulate and test hypotheses in a laboratory. They used their laboratories for dissec-

179

tion and for controlled observation, but for a long time their true laboratory remained the outdoors where living things exist in their natural surroundings. They would track down specific organisms in nature, identify visible similarities and differences among living things, and, eventually, classify them into categories such as insects, birds, reptiles, fish, deciduous and nondeciduous trees, and so on. Using artificial conditions to observe something in the laboratory that might not happen in nature was considered inappropriate. Graham Allen, a historian of modern biology, points out that the biologist-as-naturalist might have recognized that plant seedlings need sunlight to germinate, but would not have experimented to find out how much sunlight they need by taking one group out of the sun, placing a second group in the sun for a timed exposure, and measuring the differences in growth between the two.

One reason for not experimenting stemmed from a naturalist tradition that can be traced back to Aristotle. Another was the lack of techniques and equipment for undertaking experiments. For a very long time, biologists could examine only the organs and tissues visible to the naked eye and, later, cells visible through a microscope. Since smaller elements of biology could not be seen, they remained unknown. It wasn't until the development of modern laboratory technologies that biologists were able to begin to understand the finer details and even the biochemical basis of life.

Still, even before the use of mathematics and sophisticated experimentation, there were giants of innovation and imagination in biology, including the most famous biologist of all, Charles Darwin. Using the world as his laboratory, Darwin did more to popularize biology and to stimulate further research than perhaps any other biologist. He was intrigued by similarities between and variations within living species, and after two decades of observation and thought he published his hypothesis for the origin of these similarities and variations, which we refer to as the Darwinian theory of evolution.

The Work of Charles Darwin

Darwin's parents had wanted their son to be a doctor or, failing that, a clergyman, but he was determined to explore the world of nature. After completing the traditional coursework in biology, he embarked on 20 years of observation from which he derived his now-famous theory of natural selection: Since plant and animal species have the potential to multiply faster than they actually do, a "struggle for existence" must keep them from multiplying into infinitely large numbers. This struggle, he surmised, was a natural process that resulted in the elimination of the weak, rather than the strong. Thus, the fittest, as Darwin described them, would survive in greater numbers and the species would become better and better adapted to its environment over time.

Darwin was able to observe in barnyard species and, especially in the pigeons with which he worked, that populations contained significant variation in form—like size and pigmentation in animals, shape and color in plants—and that these variations were often inheritable. Farmers and plant and animal breeders had understood this phenomenon for thousands of years and applied it by allowing only recognizably useful varieties to breed. They were using what is now termed "artificial selection," since the breeder who did the selecting was an "unnatural" selective force. Therefore, Darwin could readily demonstrate variation in barnyard species.

But did variation exist in the wild and did this imply that some sort of nonartificial, or "natural," selection process was at work? If so, natural selection might be responsible for the evolutionary shaping of simpler species into complex and more "advanced" ones. But that raised still other questions that were even more difficult to answer: What was the force in nature that played the role of the breeder in the barnyard? Were there great enough variation and strong enough forces to result in the crossover from one species to another? Answers to these questions became the essence of Darwin's theory: The evolutionary change in species came through a natural selection process, fueled by a struggle for survival in an environment that, in time, would favor one variation over another.

Biology Since Darwin

While the hypotheses suggested by Darwin's work have kept scientists busy ever since, few of his ideas were easy to test during his lifetime. The results of natural selection were thought to take much too long to be observed. At that time, there was no way to speed up that evolutionary process or to recognize small changes in the wild. But if the biologists of Darwin's day had had a better understanding of genetics, they might have realized that evolution could be observed in "real" time in a fast-growing species under controlled conditions.

Discovering Evolution and Microbiology

Stephen T. Abedon, a graduate student in microbiology, is taking part in the continuing exploration of some of the questions about evolution that Darwin left unanswered.

Steve majored in science at a large state university in the East before going to the Southwest in 1984 to do graduate work. His undergraduate degree is in biochemistry, an excellent general science background that included courses in inorganic and organic chemistry, biochemistry, biology, human anatomy, human physiology, college mathematics including calculus and statistics, and computer science. In graduate school he's learned about genetics and evolutionary biology.

Steve did not always want to be in microbiology. In fact, he did not know exactly what he wanted to do in science until he started a two-year master's program in nutritional biochemistry at the university where he is now a doctoral candidate. The "wrong" choice of nutrition, however, gave him some invaluable knowledge about what he didn't want from graduate school as well as a chance to search for what he did. A single course in evolutionary biology led him to microbiology and evolutionary biology just nine months after he arrived.

Darwin's Unanswered Questions

Steve learned in his evolutionary biology course that Darwin had left several important questions unanswered. Darwin believed that evolution arose out of the twin mechanisms of variation and selection, but he could not answer fundamental questions such as: How does variation arise? How is variation transmitted? What makes variations persist? How can one apparently random genetic change not be lost among 40,000 or 400,000 plants or animals and, eventually, take over, that is, change, the species as a whole?

Mutation, an accidental change in the inheritable material, explains how variation occurs. However, mutation and how it is transmitted were not completely understood until twentieth-century biologists finally understood the nature of DNA and its role in cells. The answer to the third question, how variation persists without being overwhelmed, turned out to be a mathematical, indeed, a probabilistic, problem. A Bavarian monk, Gregor Mendel, had actually worked out the "rules" of transmission and persistence in Darwin's time, but his research was far too advanced to be understood and its significance was not realized until genetics came to be studied systematically at the beginning of this century. Thus, the story of the mathematization of biology really begins with Mendel.

Mendel's Experiments

In science, posing a different question is often what contributes to progress. Darwin focused his inquiries on what *caused* variation in nature; Gregor Mendel focused his on a subtly different question: What makes certain variations *persist*?

Mendel's method was highly experimental and mathematical, and went far beyond what could be learned through the random observation of natural populations. Mendel saw in his experimental pea patch precisely what could not be seen in nature: Inheritable but recessive characteristics, as he would call them, could be masked (hidden) in certain offspring and only show up in later generations. He chose the common garden pea as his experimental subject. By carefully controlling fertilization between peas of different and similar visible characteristics and by keeping very accurate descriptions and counts of his pea progeny, Mendel developed the notion of dominant and recessive traits and the laws that govern the mathematical ratios between them.

As Mendel discovered, if you cross (mate) a pure line of yellow pea plants with a pure line of green pea plants (yellow seed color being a dominant trait and green seed color a recessive), all the offspring in the first generation will have the same color peas: yellow. But the gene for green peas does not disappear. It is simply masked and may be "unmasked" in a later generation. In fact, in the second generation, if plants grown from the yellow pea progeny are self-fertilized, the plants will produce both yellow and green seeds in a ratio of three to one respectively, but half the seeds will

Figure 66. Mendel's Experiment

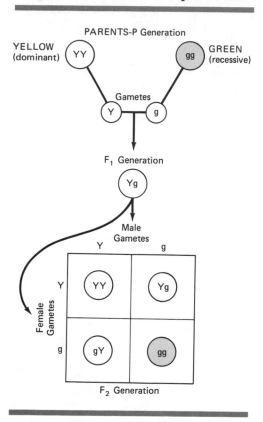

not be genetically pure. Some will be pure yellow, expressed in common genotype notation as YY; some will be pure green (gg); some will appear to be yellow but actually be genetically mixed, expressed as Yg.

Thus, in addition to conceptualizing dominant and recessive, Mendel discovered a constant ratio between dominant and recessive traits in the third generation. He was an experimentalist in the modern sense in that he kept careful count of his results. As Table 32 indicates, these visible traits tended to converge on a three-to-one ratio in the resulting plants, which is the result of genotypes in a ratio of 1:2:1.

Even more significant than the mathematical analysis of the genetics of pea traits was Mendel's demonstration that different

Table 32. Mendel's Table of Experimental Data

Dominant Trait	Number	Recessive Trait	Number	Ratio
Round seed	5,474	Wrinkled	1,850	2.9:1
Yellow seed	6,022	Green seed	2,001	3.0:1
Purple flower	705	White flower	224	3.1:1
Tall plant	787	Short plant	277	2.8:1

characteristics in nature did not *blend* genetically as had been previously thought. Here, too, was an answer to Darwin's question of how variations *persist* in very large populations. From Mendel's peas, it was obvious that spontaneous variation in nature would not necessarily disappear even if it occurred in only a few individuals and even if it were not immediately observable. Though the gene for purple-colored pea flowers is dominant, some number of white flowers show up in generation after generation as plant parents carrying *recessive* white-flower genes cross with one another. In fact, if the recessive white-flower gene were better adapted to its environment than the purple-flower gene, natural selection would favor the white-flower gene, even though it is recessive, increasing its representation in the population. Since Darwin's theory is based on variations being sustained through heredity, Mendel's work gave it much more credence. Even more important for us here, Mendel's work introduced the idea of frequency distribution in populations of organisms, what Mendel called "mathematical laws of assortment."

The Road to Population Genetics

Hardy-Weinberg Law

Several more discoveries were needed to shift the evolutionists' focus from change in individual organisms to mathematically predictable changes in populations as a whole.

The next breakthrough came when two scientists, one a mathematician, G. H. Hardy, the other a medical doctor, Wilhelm Weinberg, each working independently, observed that the kind of gene ratios Mendel had observed in his controlled populations could be predicted in nature over time, given the laws of probabilities.

Imagine a hypothetical glass jar containing an equal proportion (.50 and .50) of an *infinite* number of individual seed color genes, each either a yellow (Y) or a green (g). Now imagine that we are no longer in Mendel's controlled pea patch but rather in the natural world where genes combine by chance, that is, randomly or by some probabilistic prediction.

Now imagine reaching into the jar and picking out a gene at random. The chances of selecting a yellow gene (Y) are 50 percent, since half the genes are yellow. And the chances of selecting a green gene (g) are also 50 percent. To calculate the probability of *two* yellow genes (YY) or *two* green genes (gg) being selected simultaneously we multiply 50 percent by 50 percent for a *combined* probability of .25 (.50 × .50 = .25).

The reason that the chance of selecting a second Y or g gene is the same as the chance of selecting a first Y or g gene is that the two consecutive selections are independent events. One does not affect the other. You might compare this to tossing a penny. The chance for heads is 50 percent on every throw because previous throws do not affect subsequent ones. It is only when you try to calculate the probability of *compound* tosses that the percentage goes below 50 percent: .25 (.50 × .50) for two heads in two tosses; .125 (.50 × .50 × .50) for three heads in three tosses; and .0625 (.50 × .50 × .50 × .50) for four heads in four tosses.

In the case of the Yg or gY genotype, there is double the likelihood of picking one of each, yielding a combined probability of .50. Here is a summary of these probabilities:

> The chance of selecting YY (on two picks) is .25 (.50 × .50).
> The chance of selecting gg (on two picks) is .25 (.50 × .50).
> The sum of the probabilities of selecting Yg (gY) on two picks is .50: (.50 × .50 = .25) + (.50 × .50 = .25) = .50.

Notice that even though we are looking at random choices, we are still coming up with a 1:2:1 ratio of genotypes, the same ratio of pure yellow, mixed yellow and green, and pure green that Mendel came up with in his controlled pea patch. But what happens when the ratios of yellow and green genes in the natural population are *not* neatly 50:50? Imagine a second jar full of an infinite number of genes that are in a 70:30 ratio of the two types. In such a population where 70 percent of the genes were yellow and 30 percent green, random mating would produce the following probabilities:

> The chance of selecting a Y gene on the first try is .70.
> The chance of selecting a Y gene on the second try is .70.
> Therefore, the chance of selecting Y genes in two consecutive picks is .70 × .70 = .49.

> The chance of selecting a g gene on the first try is .30.
> The chance of selecting a g gene on the second try is .30.
> Therefore, the chance of selecting g genes in two consecutive picks is .30 × .30 = .09.

So much for producing genetically pure peas. What about the mixed variety?

> The chance of selecting a Y on the first try and a g on the second try is .70 × .30 = .21.
> The chance of selecting a g on the first try and a Y on the second try is .30 × .70 = .21.
> And the sum of these probabilities is .21 + .21 = .42.

So, starting from a seemingly more complex assortment of 70 percent yellow genes and 30 percent green genes, the following breakdown can be *predicted*.

.49 YY

.42 Yg (gY)

.09 gg

In the same way, the specific probability of trait inheritance can always be predicted as long as we know the proportions of each gene (the gene frequencies) within the infinite supply.

Now, let's do what mathematicians like to do best: generalize from our specific examples. Go back to the imagined gene jar again and instead of assigning particular ratios, like 50:50 or 70:30, let's say our jar contains p, meaning a certain fraction, of gene Y, and q, meaning another fraction of gene g. Just as 0.50 and 0.50 add up to the total in the first example, and 0.70 and 0.30 add up to the total in the second example, p and q add up to the total of 1 (i.e., 100 percent).

Now, the probability of picking out the Y gene is p. And the probability of picking two Ys in two successive tries is $p \times p$ or, as we would write it in algebraic notation, p^2. The logic remains the same if we substitute generalized terms like p and q for specific percentages in our previous examples. Thus, the probability of picking out the g gene on two successive tries is q^2.

What is the probability of producing a genetically mixed variety, picking a Y gene at p percentage and, on the second try, a g gene at q percentage (or vice versa)? Not surprisingly, the mixed variety will appear in our notation as pq (or qp). Doubling this term (because pq and qp produce the equivalent hybrid), the probability of selecting that mix is $2pq$ (Yg and gY). We end up with a generalized formula for trait distribution that looks like this:

$$p^2 + 2pq + q^2 = 1.$$

What we have now is an abstract mathematical statement that reflects a truth in nature. The statement itself is obvious mathematically because once you begin with $p + q = 1$ and square that expression, $(p + q)^2 = p^2 + 2pq + q^2$ is a straightforward exercise in algebra. But its application to biology represented a major contribution of Hardy and Weinberg. What they gave us was a profound understanding of genetic frequencies in nature. As long as we know the proportionality of genes in an infinite population, that is, that one gene is p percent of the total and another is q percent of the total, we can predict, the proportionality of the progeny. That relationship will be

$$p^2 + 2pq + q^2 = 1.$$

Populations of Genes

Hardy's and Weinberg's findings gave biologists a way to think more systematically about the random selection of inheritable traits in very large populations. Since genes are selected by chance, and chance follows certain laws of probability, the study of evolution and genetics increasingly required the aid of mathematics.

Gone are the days of simple note-taking and observation in biology. The work of modern-day biologists takes place to a much greater extent in the laboratory and at the computer as well as in the field. The evolutionary biologist has to understand mathematically how selection is related to population growth—not simply how much variation is visible, but how much is actually present, and how change in gene frequencies (evolution) takes place over time.

Becoming a Microbiologist

Steve's next step toward a Ph.D. in microbiology was to locate a university laboratory in which he could work under a senior researcher's supervision. He needed a lab in which a single research area had been fairly well defined and where an additional hard-working graduate student, like himself, could explore a related topic on his own. Every graduate student in experimental science has to become part of a team made up of a senior professor, post-doctoral students, graduate students, and lab technicians. While everyone in the lab has his or her own series of experiments to develop, there is a substantial overlapping of interests and someone is always available to respond to the call: "Hey, come over and take a look at my data. What do you make of this?" While new graduate students are encouraged to work independently, they are not likely to go far astray with experienced co-workers nearby.

The only problem with working as part of a team is that the graduate student first has to find one that fits his or her research interests. By interviewing a number of lab directors and their graduate and post-graduate assistants, Steve found that he would be able to investigate some aspect of the evolution of microorganisms in Dr. Harris Bernstein's lab.

Questions About Sexual Reproduction

Dr. Bernstein is trying to learn why sexual reproduction is so prevalent in the natural world—an important unanswered question in evolutionary biology. Nonsexual reproduction has some real advantages biologically. It is efficient in that the parent does not require a mate (a time-saving advantage) and guarantees that the single parent's genes will be represented maximally in the progeny— a clear evolutionary advantage. If the parent is well adapted to its particular environment, the offspring—perfect copies of the parent—will be well adapted, too. Despite these advantages, however, few organisms reproduce this way. Why is this? Why has sexual reproduction, which combines genetic material from two different sources, tended to prevail?

The answer, Dr. Bernstein and his colleagues believe, is that the extra genetic material provided by sexual reproduction may allow for repair of damaged DNA. A basic way for microorganisms to repair their DNA is through a process called *recombinational repair.* For this to take place, there must be extra DNA material (called DNA redundancy) accessible to the organism. Redundancy may be found within the cell of the organism or within the population of cells. The problem with providing DNA redundancy within the cell is that there would have to be at least twice as much DNA material as is necessary for normal cellular functioning. Dr. Bernstein and his colleagues believe that sexual reproduction is advantageous for microorganisms (and presumably for higher organisms as well) because it eliminates the need for DNA redundancy within the cell by providing for it within the population as a whole.

Steve's Experiments

Steve's special project has some bearing on the larger questions that Dr. Bernstein and his colleagues are trying to answer. Steve wants to test Dr. Bernstein's hypothesis that sexual reproduction is a selective advantage to organisms that have damaged DNA but a disadvantage to those that do not. To do this, he will be experimenting on microorganisms called T4 phage.

Phage are viruses that live off bacteria. In fact, every known bacterium has its own specific phage. What's interesting about phage, and viruses in general, is that before they have invaded their host bacteria they behave like nonliving substances. Yet, under the right conditions, phage will enter a specific bacterium and, within seconds, begin to multiply, behaving metabolically and reproductively like living things. T4 phage is particularly useful in microbiology research because it is simple (as far as its life cycle and DNA), and convenient to use in a laboratory setting. Because T4 has a life cycle of about 20 minutes, Steve's experiments yield the evolutionary information he needs in days instead of weeks, months, or even years.

Steve's experiments require a two-step cultivation. First, he has to grow bacteria in large quantities (in the hundreds of millions) and under controlled conditions. Then he has to add similarly large quantities of phage and "infect" his bacterial cultures.

T4 phage consists mostly of DNA surrounded by a protein shell. The DNA contains a code to construct many gene products: One, called the *imm* gene (for immunity), comes in two varieties. The more common form is *imm*$^+$ and it prevents sexual reproduction by causing a barrier to form around the bacterial cell it has infected, keeping out any other phage. The second, less common form is *imm*$^-$ and its genetic information contains no code for a barrier. Thus it permits or, as biologists would put it, favors sexual reproduction.

All of this activity is another variation of the struggle for existence Darwin noted more than a century ago. If the phage can put a barrier around the bacteria cell, it is able to fence itself in, so to speak, and will not have to share its resources with other, competing phage, which eliminates a "cost" of sex. If other phage got in, the first phage would parent fewer of the resulting offspring.

There was no way Mendel could know whether there were recessive genes in his hybrid pea plants, except to control their mating and carefully examine the next generation. Testing offspring is one way experimental biologists confirm the presence or absence of certain genes in the parent population. And that is precisely what Steve is going to do: test the offspring of his various phage-bacteria infections to see which type was favored in this short-term evolution of their species.

Steve wants to find out whether DNA damage in phage selects for *imm*$^-$, favoring sexual reproduction. To do this, he will have to show that *imm*$^-$ phage have a greater chance for survival than *imm*$^+$ where there is DNA damage. If he succeeds in demonstrating a correlation between the selection for *imm*$^-$ phage and the presence of DNA damage, he will have added support to Dr. Bernstein's theory that sex is advantageous due to its help in repairing DNA damage. But first he must undertake a control experiment using undamaged phage. He needs to show that sexual reproduction truly does *not* take place with undamaged *imm*$^+$ phage populations but *does* take place with undamaged *imm*$^-$ populations in order to show that sexual reproduction or the absence thereof in the T4 system is consistent with other systems. Then, he will experiment with *damaged imm⁺* and *imm⁻* phage populations and compare the results with those from the control group. The hypothesis of Steve's control experiment is that one variety of the *imm* gene will produce a barrier that prevents secondary infection and the other variety will not.

Steve's experiments, then, are going to involve a series of intentional infections of bacterial cultures by *genetically different* stocks of T4 phage. Working with the fast-reproducing virus permits him to observe changes in gene frequency over time—evolution—in a very short period of time.

Figure 67 shows the sequence of Steve's experiment. There are two conditions and two stages of infection. If the primary infection consists of just *imm⁺*, secondary phage will not get in because a barrier will be in place (Condition A). If the primary infection, however, consists of just *imm⁻*, secondary phage will get in (Condition B). Steve observes these effects by noting whether or not secondary phage show up in the offspring after one 20-minute generation.

Figure 67

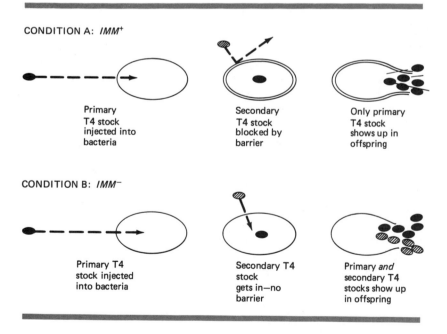

CONDITION A: *IMM⁺*

Primary
T4 stock
injected into
bacteria

Secondary
T4 stock
blocked by
barrier

Only primary
T4 stock
shows up in
offspring

CONDITION B: *IMM⁻*

Primary T4
stock injected
into bacteria

Secondary T4
stock
gets in—no
barrier

Primary *and*
secondary T4
stocks show up
in offspring

Predicting Results

Among the problems Steve had to solve before undertaking his experiments was how to *predict* the expected results. If he could begin with a prediction of what should occur if the hypothesis were correct, then all he would have to do is compare the results of his experiments with his prediction, and he would have a finding to report to the scientific community at large.

But how to make that prediction? That is where mathematical modeling comes in. Steve had to construct an equation that defined mathematically the expected experimental outcomes under various conditions.

There are some general similarities in method between Steve's experiment in microbiology and Dr. MacCorquodale's social-science research. The notion of significant difference plays a part in both cases; here the question is whether the experiments with imm^+ and imm^- produce significantly different results. Expectancies have to be defined and then compared to outcomes, just as in the chi-square test. A null hypothesis is also implied here; Steve must demonstrate that the differences he finds could not have happened by chance.

Constructing the Right Equation

Steve constructed the following equation to use as a predictor in his experiment with T4 phage.[1]

$$P = \sum_{i=1}^{m} \sum_{j=1}^{n} \frac{A^i e^{-A}}{i!} \frac{B^j e^{-B}}{j!} \frac{i}{i + Ej}$$

There are a number of ways to tackle a long equation like this one. We can start by trying to figure out which are the variables and which the constants in the equation. We can take its elements apart, mathematical expression by mathematical expression, and try to make sense of each of them in turn. Or, we can stand back from

---

1. This particular model is of the control experiment using undamaged phage. A similar but more complicated equation generates expectancies in the experiments with damaged phage, but it will not be presented here.

the equation and try to see the connection between the theory on which the experiment is based and its mathematical model.

Let's try to do all three, one at a time, starting with the connection between the theory and the model. Translated into words, what is the equation trying to tell us?

> *P is the predicted* ratio *of phage offspring from the primary infection (i) to the total number of offspring (i + j) after one generation has reproduced. That ratio will depend on whether or not a barrier* E *blocking out the secondary infection was in place.*

The terms primary infection, secondary infection, imm^+, and imm^- aren't included in the equation, even though we know these are factors in the experiment, because Steve has translated them into abstract mathematical expressions. The equation is to be a *model* of what he expects to occur, based on theory, and the results of his experiment will be compared to his theoretical value, *P*.

The only real unknown is *P*. The letters *A* and *B* in the equation are variables that will change each time the experiment is performed and they represent proportions of real, measurable quantities of phage and real measurable quantities of bacteria. *A* is the ratio of the total number of primarily infected phage to the total number of bacterial cells, and *B* is the ratio of the total number of secondarily infected phage to the total number of bacterial cells. So *A* and *B* represent similar kinds of proportions that are neither conceptually nor technically difficult to obtain. And *e*, you may recall, is an irrational number that equals 2.1718 . . . .

But the proportions of *total* phage to bacteria don't tell Steve the number of phage infections in any one particular bacterial cell. A single bacterium can host many more than one phage and as few as none, so how is Steve going to get a feel for the *likely distributions* of phage in each infection?

Using Poisson Distribution

Think of the problem this way. If you had a certain number of marbles you were throwing at a certain number of cans, you could easily calculate the *average* number of marbles that you could get into a can (*A* and *B* in Steve's equation). But, how would you know,

Figure 68. Possible Distributions of Phage

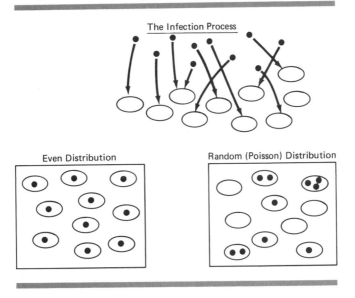

The Infection Process

Even Distribution

Random (Poisson) Distribution

or even reasonably guess, how many marbles would land in any particular can (*i* and *j* in Steve's equation)? Steve knows that it is unlikely that the phage would distribute themselves exactly evenly in each infection. So he chooses a Poisson distribution, the distribution law concerned with the occurrence of a small number of events in random sampling processes. Using Poisson distribution, Steve can figure out for every value of *A* or *B*, what the *likely* distribution of phage might be at the level of the individual cell.

You don't have to know where the Poisson distribution comes from in order to use it. The Poisson distribution formula helps the experimenter calculate the proportion of bacterial cells that are likely to have a certain number of infecting phage. The entire middle section of Steve's equation is taken up with figuring out those likelihoods by means of Poisson distributions for primary infections (*A* and *i*) and for secondary infections (*B* and *j*).

$$P = \sum_{i=1}^{m} \sum_{j=1}^{n} \frac{A^i e^{-A}}{i!} \frac{B^j e^{-B}}{j!} \frac{i}{i + Ej}$$

Let's put some simple numbers into the first expression (for A and i) and see how a Poisson distribution works.

$$\frac{A^i e^{-A}}{i!}$$

A is the ratio of total phage to total bacteria in the first infection and i is a possible number of phage per individual bacterium. Let's say that A is 5, which means that on the average there will be 5 phage for every bacterium. What the Poisson distribution formula answers is the question: Given an overall 5:1 ratio of phage to bacteria, what is the *fraction* of the total population of bacteria that will have, for example, 4 phage per cell? This is how that answer is found for $A = 5; i = 4$.

$$\frac{A^i e^{-A}}{i!}$$

In words, this would be A raised to the i power times e raised to the minus-A power and the whole quantity divided by i factorial.

$$\frac{5^4 e^{-5}}{4!} = \frac{625 e^{-5}}{24}$$

The calculator tells us that $e^{-5} = .0067$ and that $4! = 24$. By completing the arithmetic we find that approximately 17.55 percent of the bacterial population is likely to host 4 phage each, given a ratio of total phage to bacteria of 5.

By testing all reasonable values of i (and later j) in terms of all reasonable values of A (and later B), Steve will have a series of probabilities with which he can calculate the numerical outcomes of his *imm*$-$ and *imm*$+$ infections.

The terms i and j in the Poisson distribution expression are defined by the summation expression and therefore represent a series of changing values. Steve has to consider all individual possibilities of i and j, and then multiply the expected ratio of i to total phage by the *probability* of a given i and j occurring. This is called a *weighted average* and is necessary because phage are not evenly distributed over the entire population of bacteria.

The power of the Poisson distribution is that it gives the re-

Table 33. Poisson Distribution for Phage into Bacteria Where Total Average (A) = 5

i	A^i	$i!$	$\dfrac{A^i e^{-A}}{i!}$	
i = 0	1	1	0.006738	0.67%
i = 1	5	1	0.0336?	3.37%
i = 2	25	2	0.08423	8.42%
i = 3	125	6	0.1404	14.04%
i = 4	625	24	0.1755	17.55%
i = 5	3,125	120	0.1755	17.55%
i = 6	15,625	720	0.1462	14.62%
i = 7	78,125	5,040	0.1044	10.44%
i = 8	390,625	40,320	0.0693	6.93%
i = 9	1,953,125	362,880	0.0363	3.63%
i = 10	9,765,625	3,628,800	0.0181	1.81%

searcher a way of systematically considering all random distributions when it is impossible to count the actual outcomes (see Table 33). The figures in the last column are the percentages of bacteria likely to be infected by the number of phage in the first column; for example, the probability that there will be 4 phage per bacteria (look at the $i = 4$ row above) is 17.55 percent; the probability there will be 10 phage per bacteria is 1.81 percent; and so on. When you graph these percentages (see Figure 69) the resulting curve forms a distribution similar to the normal distribution we encountered on page 124.

Just as the expression

$$\frac{A^i e^{-A}}{i!}$$

represented the Poisson distribution formula for A and i (the initial infection), so the expression

$$\frac{B^j e^{-B}}{j!}$$

represents the Poisson distribution formula for B and j (the secondary infection).

Now we are ready to look at the last term in Steve's equation.

$$P = \sum_{i=1}^{m} \sum_{j=1}^{n} \frac{A^i e^{-A}}{i!} \frac{B^j e^{-B}}{j!} \overbrace{\frac{i}{i + Ej}}$$

If i is the number of phage resulting from the primary infection of a bacterial cell and j the number of phage in the same cell as a result of the secondary infection, then

$$\frac{i}{i + Ej}$$

is the proportion of offspring of the primary phage over the total phage population. What Steve wants to be able to demonstrate in the last expression of his equation is the actual representation among the offspring of the primary phage type, given specific values of i and j.

Creating the Key Mathematical Term

How he does this mathematically is perhaps the most creative aspect of Steve's model. He uses a term he designates E, to which he assigns only one of two values: either $E = 1$ (meaning all secondary phage got in) or $E = 0$ (meaning no secondary phage got in). The E term can be thought of as a kind of door. Either the door is open ($E = 1$) or the door is closed ($E = 0$). See how these two values of E affect the last expression in Steve's equation:
If $E = 1$, we have

$$\frac{i}{i + Ej} = \frac{i}{i + (1)j} = \frac{i}{i + j}.$$

If $E = 0$, we have

$$\frac{i}{i + Ej} = \frac{i}{i + (0)j} = \frac{i}{i}.$$

The j term has disappeared where $E = 0$ because any number and, therefore, any variable multiplied by 0 equals 0.

The use of the E term gets us right to the heart of mathematical modeling. With E, Steve has created a mathematical term that

Figure 69. Poisson Distribution for Phage Into Bacteria Where Total Average (A) = 5

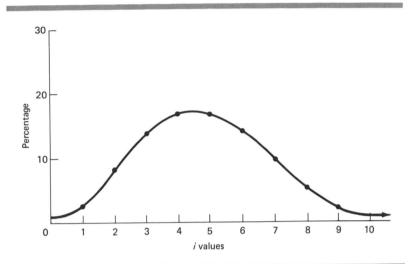

represents the biological phenomenon of the barrier. It is a simple term, having only two conditions (or states), 1 or 0; but it can model what is likely to be going on within a particular bacterial cell that has been infected with primary phage of quantity i and secondary phage of quantity j.

While the E term may seem simplistic, it has the potential to describe a natural event and it forms the basis for the much more complex equation that deals with the effect of DNA damage on infections of imm^+ and imm^- phage.

In more advanced mathematics, you will be introduced to the specific techniques Steve is using in this equation to generate different i and j values and to calculate their probabilities. With those standard techniques, Steve is able to hypothesize certain values of i and j from 1 to m or n, work out the probabilities of any one of those values occurring, and then plug in the open door/closed door E term that forms the theoretical basis of his work. Steve's equation is a good example of the utility of mathematics in today's scientific research since it is through such models that a quantitative understanding of natural phenomena is possible.

Chapter

9

Economics and Business: Planning for Profits

You won't be surprised to learn that economics and business require some familiarity with mathematics. After all, economics deals with the values by which goods and services are measured, and the bottom line in business is money. While accounting consists mainly of arithmetic calculations of income and expenses, modern businesses use much more sophisticated mathematics to plan and assess the profitability of what they do. We have already seen how linear programming helps managers plan optimally. In this chapter, we will see why calculus and even mathematical models have become essential to money-based activities.

The Founders of Economics

Adam Smith was the first modern economist. While he did not use a mathematical approach to the subject, his insights led thinkers after him to reconsider the meaning of "wealth." Smith lived during the late eighteenth century, just after the period when Spain, Portugal, England, and Holland had completed their exploitation of the New World. He noticed and was the first to explain why the tremendous wealth that Spain had gained from the shiploads of gold, furs, and silver that came from the Americas had been lost within 150 years, while England, which had concentrated instead on colonizing the New World, was getting richer all the time.

Smith was convinced that a nation's wealth was not the amount of gold or other precious metals in its treasuries, but its capacity to produce more wealth: its land, manufactured products, commerce, workforce, and (though Smith didn't mention this at the time, he might have included it if he were writing today), educational system which guarantees technological innovation into the future. The difference between England's and Spain's economies was that England had put the wealth received from the New World to work and in so doing, had multiplied its value many times over. Money stored in warehouses wasn't put to use, Smith said, but money invested in active trade and manufacturing was.

The next economist to build on Smith's analysis was David Ricardo, another Englishman, writing soon after Smith. Ricardo went beyond Smith in questioning what the variables are in a nation's economy that produce wealth. He came up with three: profits, wages, and rent. Profit was the value that the investor or business owner gained from the use of his money; wages were the value the laborer gained from the use of his hands; rent was the value the property owner gained from the land that he let others use for planting or grazing. Underlying all of this was Ricardo's search for a fundamental meaning of value. He questioned what makes something valuable apart from extreme scarcity (diamonds) and extreme utility (water), and what makes values change.

Mathematizing Economics: Marginalism

The next great leap toward mathematizing economics came with the so-called marginalist theories developed between 1870 and 1914. The marginalists approached economic analysis in a more mathematical and specific way than earlier economists had. Instead of looking at the economy of a nation, as Smith and Ricardo had (now called macroeconomics), the marginalists studied the economics of individual enterprises (microeconomics) and even the economics of a single decision to purchase. Their main contribution, mathematically, was the concept of *marginalism* for which the entire group is named.

Marginal Utility

Marginalism focuses on how resources are allocated, whether those resources are the productive capacity of a large manufacturing firm, the dollars on deposit that a bank may invest, or your own money and time. Suppose you were crazy about ice cream and were offered unlimited scoops at a very low price. At first you would gladly pay the price for this desirable product, but eventually, when you'd had so much ice cream that it had no more appeal, it would not be worth even the pennies you were paying to eat another scoop.

The "value" of the first scoop would be worth a lot to you; the second scoop, a little less. By the time you were offered the tenth scoop, the value of that additional serving might be close to zero. The scoops of ice cream, the economist would say, have *diminishing marginal utility* for you, meaning that the value of ice cream (and most other products) is reduced with each additional purchase.

Let's put some numbers into this example. Suppose the unlimited scoops were offered to you for $.50 each. The first scoop of ice cream might actually be worth $1 to you, so you would consider it a bargain at $.50. The next scoop might be worth perhaps $.90 to you, so the $.50 price would still be appealing. You would probably continue buying the ice cream until a scoop was worth no more than $.50 to you. Then it would no longer be a bargain. If you turned down the next scoop, you would have made a decision *at the margin*. The point is—and the marginalists were the first to quantify this—most rational beings will stop buying a product like ice cream when the value of the *marginal utility* of the last scoop equals the *marginal cost* of the next scoop, because individuals want to allocate their income efficiently between ice cream and dollars, and there are an awful lot of things you can do with your money besides buy ice cream.

To take another example, imagine you were asked to work overtime at a pay rate of time and a half. Would you work until you were exhausted? Perhaps at the beginning you would because you wanted the money to buy a compact disc player and the additional earnings would mean a lot to you. But, at some point, the *utility,* or value, of the additional wages of one more hour of overtime work would be lessened. You would have most of the money you wanted, and you would begin to prefer allocating your time resource to leisure (sports and play) than to still more work. This, too, reflects decision making at the margin. As you earn more money, your desire for more overtime work will diminish.

You make decisions at the margin every day. You decide to buy a cheaper VCR, though the more expensive one is tempting, because the added cost of extra features will not compensate for the loss of either leisure time—your having to work more to pay for the VCR—or the new skis you would then not be able to afford. The marginalists believed that businesses, like individuals, allocate their resources rationally in order to stay in a balanced position between having just so much of one item so as not to cheat themselves of just so much of another.

Mathematics became useful to the marginalists because they were trying to locate the exact point at which the marginal utility of one activity or purchase equals the marginal utility of another, and this concept can best be understood and applied by means of calculus.

Measuring Slopes: The Way to Calculus in Economics

Very often consumers, whether they are individuals or organizations, have a number of combinations of options that will satisfy them and have no strong preference for one option or another. As economists would put it, they are "indifferent." A college student, with limited resources, may have to weigh the size of an off-campus apartment against its distance from the campus. The farther away from school, the larger the apartment, for the same rental cost. But distance from school may require the purchase of a car. If several combinations of size, nearness to school, and cost will equally satisfy the college student's needs, he or she can be said to be indifferent to which combination is chosen.

To take another example, faced with the need for additional urban transportation, a city planning board may be indifferent to whether they contract for so many miles of light-rail mass transit, or so many miles of new highway, or some combination of the two.

Plotting an Indifference Curve

Imagine that you are the head of a committee planning a school party for 100 people. You have learned that you can hire a band at a certain price per musician and you can buy drinks and food at a certain price per serving. The utility that you want to maximize in this case is having a good time. You and your committee know that certain combinations of entertainment and refreshments will guarantee that good time. If you hire a single electric guitarist, you're going to have to provide a lot of drinks and food. If you get a seven-piece band, you can cut down on the amount of refreshments. How are you going to decide on the right combination of food, drink, and music? Economists have a way of conceptualizing this sort of problem in terms of a *marginal rate of substitution*. If you could graph the rate of substitution between refreshments and music, you could figure out how to get the maximum good time for the lowest possible cost.

You know, from talking to your classmates, that a single guitarist is acceptable only if there is a lot of food—about two servings for each person. But if you hire a seven-piece band, people will be too busy dancing to eat much so you will need less food.

From this information you can plot an indifference curve, or what you might call a "curve of constant satisfaction," because any point along that curve reflects an equivalent amount of a good time. Figure 70 shows what an indifference curve between refreshments and musicians might look like.

The line is curved rather than straight because there isn't a constant rate of variation; one less musician doesn't mean 20 more servings at each point along the curve. If there were such a one-to-one rate of substitution, your decision would be an easy one: Using more of the cheaper item would give you the most economical party with the same total good time. Try some numbers and you'll see

Figure 70

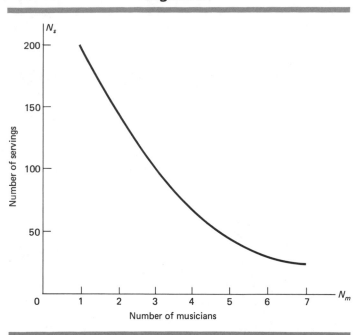

that the correspondence between band size and amount of food and drinks keeps changing along the curve.

Plotting the Price Line

Once you have your indifference curve drawn, the next step is to figure out the lowest possible cost of satisfying the guests. Start by constructing an equation to express the total cost of the party in terms of what will produce a good time. Let N stand for the number of items and P for the price per item. Use the subscript s (for serving) for the variables associated with refreshments and m for those related to the musicians. Then you can calculate the cost of refreshments by multiplying N_s by P_s and the cost of the band by multiplying N_m by P_m. The following equation expresses the total cost, C, in terms of these algebraic variables.

$$N_s P_s + N_m P_m = C$$

Getting the Most for the Least

Economists call the type of linear equation described above and its straight-line representation a "price line" or "budget line" because it reflects both the relative prices of the items available for purchase and the total amount of money the committee can spend. These values are not expressed in numbers, but in algebraic relationships. We could use the same type of equation to represent transportation options or the value of overtime wages.

Now, the object of the analysis is to find the lowest value of C that will satisfy the students' party preferences. We can do this by drawing the price line on the same graph as the indifference curve and finding the point at which they first make contact. This is not unlike trying to find the highest point in the constraint polygon for the highest profit, as we did in the chapter on linear programming. To minimize cost, we are now looking for the *lowest* point shared by the two functions—the least amount of food, drink, and music that will guarantee a good party.

Figure 71 shows five different price lines, each representing a different total amount of funds to be spent ($C_1, C_2 \ldots C_5$). Each

Figure 71

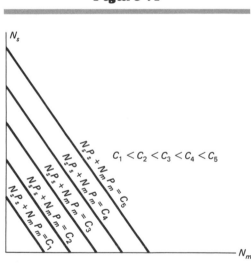

line has the same slope because each represents the same price ratio between food and drink servings (N_sP_s) and number of musicians (N_mP_m).

The next step is to plot these several different price lines on the same graph as the indifference curve in order to locate a price line (a total amount of funds) that will share at least one point (Point A in Figure 72) with the indifference curve. As you can see, the price line that is a tangent to the indifference curve is

$$N_sP_s + N_mP_m = C_3.$$

Figure 72

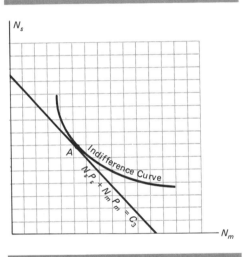

From Geometry to Calculus

Once we have a price line tangent to the indifference curve, we have a geometrical (graphic) solution to the problem of what to purchase for the party. The coordinates of point A will give us the *combination* of elements that will produce the most fun at the least cost.

But how do we quantify point A? How do we go from this rough geometric representation of the solution (which enhances our ability to think about the problem) to an actual solution in numbers?

How do we know how many musicians and how many servings of food and drink point A represents? To find out we have to apply the techniques of calculus, which provide the means of finding the value of the slope of a curve *at any point* along the curve. Since we already know the fixed slope of the price line, we want to look for the place where the slope of the curve exactly matches the slope of the line.

It might appear from the preceding graph that we *do* know the location of point A, but remember that geometry only gives us a rough location of a point. The exact value of point A can only be calculated with the help of calculus.

When you study economics, you won't have to use calculus in solving problems right away, but if you know calculus you will have a much better understanding of what is going on from the beginning. In more advanced economics, and in higher-level business analysis, you will need the kind of precise information that can only be found by using calculus.

Supply and Demand

Alfred Marshall, a key figure in the development of economics, believed that most economic phenomena could be reduced to mathematical equations. He was looking for a comprehensive way to measure the economic value of goods produced and sold. Earlier economists had defined the value of a product either in terms of the amount of effort that went into the product (the labor theory of value) or the product's "exchange value," meaning the price paid for a product when it was freely bought and sold in the market. According to the latter theory, buyers would pay only as much as an item was "worth" to them (at the margin, or course) no matter how much labor and supplies had gone into making that product. Since this worth could go up and down with scarcity and saturation (as in the ice cream and overtime-work examples), the "natural" price would fluctuate with demand and with the amount of supply.

Into the last decades of the nineteenth century, then, there were two competing theories of value and price. One held that the price of a product is set according to its cost. The other held that a product's value depends on the strength of consumer demand and that this demand can be explained by the product's *marginal utility* to the consumer. Marshall synthesized these theories. "We might as well dispute whether it is the upper- or the underblade of a pair of scissors which cuts a piece of paper as whether value is governed by utility [demand] or cost of production," Marshall wrote. Combining the labor theory of value with the exchange theory of value, he developed the idea that the price of a product (which he called the "equilibrium price") is based on supply and demand. The actual price is determined by plotting the supply curve and demand curve on a graph and locating the point at which they intersect.

Let's look at demand and supply diagrams separately and then combine them to find the equilibrium price for a common item like potato chips.

Transposing the Axes

First, a warning. For reasons that are still debated, economists defy the common convention of putting the independent variable on the *x*-axis and the dependent variable on the *y*-axis. They do just the reverse. In supply-and-demand graphs the independent variable, price, is put on the *y*-axis and the quantity is on the *x*-axis. If scientists or mathematicians were drawing these curves, they would put price on the *x*-axis to indicate that it is the variable that is changing independently, and put supply-and-demand quantities on the *y*-axis because they are a *result* of changes in price.

Figure 73 is an example of how different the same information can look on a graph when the axes are reversed. The graphs represent labor supply plotted against the price of labor or wages. The one on the left is drawn as an economist would plot the curve. The one on the right is drawn in the standard fashion. Note what has changed: only the convention as to which axis represents the independent variable and which the dependent variable. Both graphs show that, as wages increase, more workers are willing to work longer hours, up to a point. Then the curve bends backward or downward as workers have enough money and prefer more leisure time to more work.

To conform to the way economists do things, the supply-and-demand diagrams that follow will be plotted with price on the *y*-axis and supply-and-demand quantities on the *x*-axis.

Demand Diagram

The demand diagram for any product is simply a graph showing how the quantity demanded during a specified period of time will change as the price of that product changes. In the potato chip

Figure 73

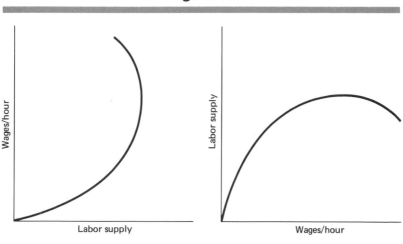

demand diagram (Figure 74), we are shown how many bags of potato chips will be demanded at each price per bag. Notice that the quantity demanded *decreases* along the x-axis as the price *increases* along the y-axis. At $3 per bag, 4 bags might be purchased, while at $1 per bag, a consumer would be tempted to buy 7.

Let's look at what happens when there is a change and consumer income increases. That means consumers have more money to spend on all purchases, including potato chips. The rise in income causes the demand curve to shift from demand 1 to demand 2. Now consumers will be willing to pay price 2 instead of price 1 for the same number of bags. What we have on the graph in Figure 75 are two parallel demand curves. At one income level, the consumer might be willing to spend only $1 for 7 bags of potato chips; at a higher income level, $2 for the same number of bags.

Figure 74. Demand Diagram

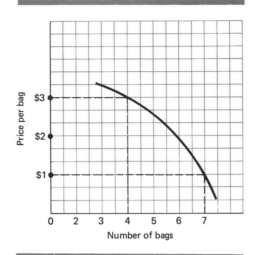

Figure 75. Demand Diagram
at Two Income Levels

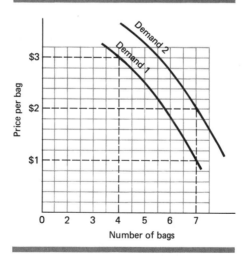

Figure 76. Supply Diagram

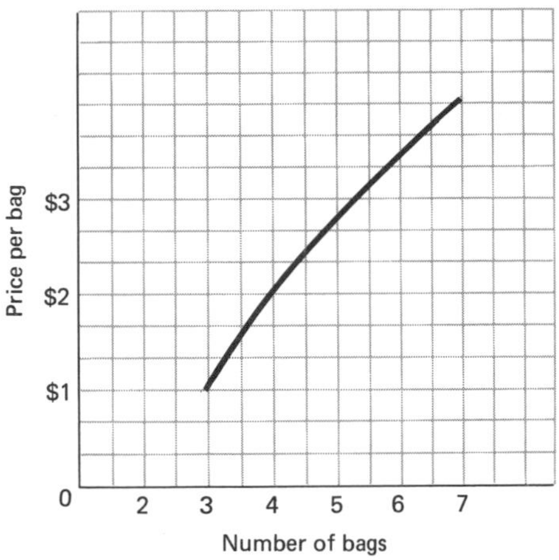

The higher the sales price, the more willing the retailer will be to sell.

Supply Diagram

Now let's look at a supply diagram for potato chips, which shows how the quantity *supplied* during a specified period will change as the price of the product changes. The supply diagram in Figure 76 shows how many bags of potato chips the producer will willingly supply at different prices. Notice that the quantities supplied *increase* when prices go up while the quantities demanded *decrease* when prices rise (see previous graphs). This makes sense since the consumer wants to save money and the producer wants to make money.

Equilibrium Price

Now that we have looked at demand and supply as functions of price, we have to combine the diagrams to find the point at which they intersect. That point identifies the price at which suppliers would be willing to sell and consumers willing to buy. In Figure 77,

Figure 77. Combined Supply and Demand

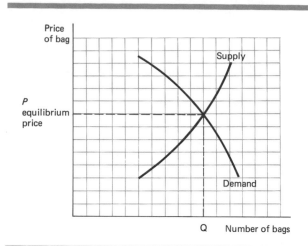

that equilibrium price is P and the equilibrium quantity is Q. This supply-demand diagram is at the heart of economics because it demonstrates the intersection of different demands and values. Today's economists use these and other quantitative methods to explain how enterprises, purchasers, investments, and even countries behave with regard to trade.

Twentieth-Century Economics

When Marshall, a mathematician by training, published his book *The Principles of Economics,* in which his theory of price equilibrium was laid out, he put his supply-and-demand diagrams into a footnote where, as economics historian Phyllis Deane puts it, "mathematically squeamish" economists could ignore them. Today, however, there is no room in economics for the mathematically squeamish. What began as a subfield of natural and social philosophy with Adam Smith has become a discipline that requires from one to three years of college mathematics.

Elasticities

Another development in economic theory that rests on mathematics is *elasticity*. Certain consumer demands are more "elastic" than others; they are more responsive to changes in consumer income. Luxury purchases tend to be eliminated when a person's income goes down because these purchases are less urgent than either food or rent. Demand for products such as new automobiles (usually a luxury item) will fluctuate more than demand for food for the same reason. At the same time, it is hard to reduce the cost of an automobile because its many parts are previously price-fixed. But prices of vegetables will vary enormously depending on the season, how far they have to be shipped, and how long refrigerated.

Externalities

Costs that are external to production, *externalities,* are other quantifiable factors related to supply, demand, and price. Economists have to deal with such questions as who should pay for the cost of dirty clothes in a coal-mining area where coal dust affects everyone's laundry. Should the townspeople absorb these costs or should the coal-mining company make a contribution? And if so, how much should that contribution be?

Externalities include such crucial aspects as the costs of disposing of toxic wastes generated by manufacturing plants, the costs of restoring strip-mined areas to prevent erosion, the costs of developing safety devices to protect people who live along rail lines where nuclear wastes are transported, and so on. And, not surprisingly, economists are regularly employed in these industries and in the federal agencies that regulate them to *think about* and *quantify* these external costs so that they can be allocated as fairly as possible among government, business, the consumer, and the tax-payer.

Whether their clients are a government agency seeking to regulate external costs or a private industry seeking to maximize profit, economists play a useful role. They are able to create models that will predict, even before management actually has to *make* a decision, what the effect of that decision will be. In the following section, we'll look at some business decisions and see how economic models, based on mathematics, can protect a business from making unwise choices and enable it to be innovative.

Mathematics and Business

Economists use math to describe the "natural" behavior of consumers, firms, and entire economies as completely as they can in order to *predict* what is going to happen next. Business is decision-oriented. So, the mathematics that is useful to business owners and managers is that which gives them some sense of the *effect* of a decision before they make it, and some way of assessing the most profitable route to follow. A number of mathematical applications have become the substance of business courses ranging from accounting and finance to marketing and strategic planning.

Production

A vast number of goods and services are part of the American economy, and decisions have to be made constantly about the optimal size of output, given plant size, labor costs, and expected sales. How does a producer decide how many items to manufacture in any one production period? It will depend on what share of the market that producer can reasonably expect to capture, the price those items can command given current supply and demand, the cost of labor and materials, and the cost of storing unsold goods. Each of these factors can be quantified based on past history and future projections, but the task of melding them into a single equation or model requires more advanced techniques.

Facing an increased demand for a product, how is the producer going to decide whether or not to meet that demand? There may be a good reason for keeping production below the maximum. Increasing production to the absolute limit of what the plant and the workforce can handle may not be wise and business managers know that maximum production and maximum profit do not always go hand in hand. If, however, all workers are fully employed and all plants operating at full capacity, management is going to have to consider expansion, which involves—even in the short run—increasing the labor force either by paying overtime or hiring temporary workers. Every business action incurs a cost. New workers will have a lower productivity level at the beginning, which increases the cost of their work. There are also costs involved in letting workers go if demand drops off. Business decisions, thus, are immediately translated into operational questions such as: What is the per-unit cost of meeting a certain amount of excess demand? At what point does maintaining the highest possible rate of profit mean *not* meeting that demand?

Such questions can best be handled mathematically. In this section, we'll look closely at a few business situations to see how mathematics can be used to describe them with great precision and to find an optimum profit-maximizing decision in each case.

Growth Curves

Lumber companies today no longer cut down entire forests. Rather, they plant trees of various kinds, maintain them, and then harvest them on a regular schedule. Calculating when and how many to cut down of each variety can be handled by mathematical models. Some of the variables that would go into the calculations include such predictable factors as the number of board feet of lumber that will be generated by each additional year of growth, as compared to the marginal cost of maintaining those trees in the forest. Other less predictable variables, such as the price of lumber in any particular time period, would also have to be included. While the mathematical models will have a number of "certainties" and "uncertainties," it's possible to determine mathematically the optimum cutting period. The most important piece of information is the *growth curve* of a particular tree.

The three graphs in Figure 78 show three different patterns of growth for a particular kind of lumber-producing tree. In each case the amount of board feet in the forest is a function of time $f(t)$, spoken f of t.

In graph A the growth curve begins rather slowly, meaning that for every year of growth up to t_1 there is only a small increase in board feet; then there is a spurt that considerably increases the amount of lumber, followed by a tapering-off period. Assuming the entire period of time is divided into four equal parts, the graph makes it clear that it would *not* be wise to cut and replant after t_1 but it would make sense to cut and replant after t_2. That way, in the same total length of time, one would get two full harvests.

In graph B, the growth curve is linear, which means that over time there is a constant rate of growth and hence a constant increase in the amount of lumber. If this were the case (though it probably

Figure 78

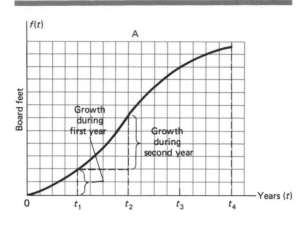

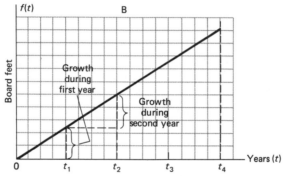

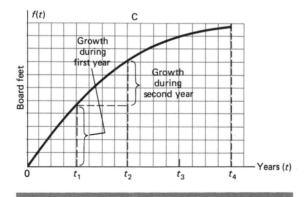

never is in the real world), the decision about when to cut would depend on other factors such as the cost of cutting versus the cost of replanting (because a replanted tree would grow just as fast as an existing one). If the cost of cutting and replanting, for example, were considerably higher than the cost of maintaining the forest, the when-to-cut decision would have a significant effect on profit. If those costs were about equal, management might be indifferent as to when to cut because the growth at the margin would equal the profit at the margin. (See p. 203 for a discussion of margins.) But, if the company wanted to get cash out of its investment in the forest, it would be advantageous to cut fairly often since no gain would be realized until a tree was felled.

In graph C, we have a different situation entirely: The most rapid rate of growth is in the first time period. After that, growth slackens and remains slow. In this instance, it would pay to cut and reforest very frequently.

Once the actual growth curve is drawn, the business planner's task is to figure out how to maximize income. Income in this instance is proportional to the yield of board feet produced by year. Since yield (the growth curve) at the end of t years is $f(t)$, then *annual* yield can be expressed mathematically as

$$\frac{f(t)}{t} \qquad \frac{\text{(total harvest)}}{\text{(total time)}}$$

and to increase income, the planner will want to maximize $f(t)/t$.

While it is technically possible to do this maximization by trial and error, the techniques of calculus are much better suited, as you discovered in the earlier problem of choosing the optimal mix of food, beverages, and music for a school party. You wanted to determine the minimum cost; the lumber company wants to ascertain the point of maximum income. The techniques for doing both are the same.

Distribution

Manufacturers often face a transportation or routing problem: how to deliver a product most efficiently from factory to receiving location. The problem will be more acute if the product is large, or cannot be stored very long, and if the delivery demands are unpredictable. Some companies, like United Parcel Service, divide cities into zones and, at the beginning of every working day, assign each driver all of the packages to be delivered in a particular zone. But have you ever wondered how those zones were initially defined so as to meet customer needs that vary from day to day? Or, how a manufacturer of cement, which must be delivered the moment it is needed, arranges trucking to a variety of building sites? To generate the most efficient delivery schedule, the business planners first have to put all of the available information into a form that can be manipulated mathematically. A cement manufacturer knows the output of each factory, the capacity of each of its trucks, and the need at each building site. The cost of transportation is proportional to the distance between the factory and each construction site, which he also knows.

Imagine, then, a cement company that has two factories (S_1 and S_2) and needs to truck cement to three different distribution sites in a single town (D_1, D_2, and D_3). The layout of the problem and the cost of transportation between the two factories and the three distribution sites are represented schematically in Figure 79.

The constraints on the problem are the amount of cement each of the two factories can produce and the specific needs of the three building sites. We don't know yet how many truckloads will be shipped, so we call this factor X_{ij} where the subscript i indicates which factory and the subscript j which distribution site.

Figure 79

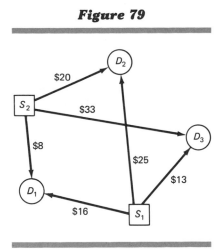

Thus we have the following distribution possibilities:

X_{11} meaning a certain number of truckloads delivering from factory 1 to destination 1

X_{12} meaning a certain number of truckloads delivering from factory 1 to destination 2

X_{13} meaning a certain number of truckloads delivering from factory 1 to destination 3

X_{21} meaning a certain number of truckloads delivering from factory 2 to destination 1

X_{22} meaning a certain number of truckloads delivering from factory 2 to destination 2

X_{23} meaning a certain number of truckloads delivering from factory 2 to destination 3

The cement factory owner wants to *minimize* the total transporation cost while making the necessary shipments. The next step in the mathematization of the problem is to add the transportation costs. Look again at Figure 79. The cost of shipment between factory 1 and destination 1 is $16; so the cost of shipping X_{11} truckloads of cement becomes $16X_{11}$. By the same logic, the cost of shipping X_{12} truckloads of cement becomes $25X_{12}$; the cost of shipping X_{13} truckloads of cement becomes $13X_{13}$; the cost of shipping X_{21} truckloads of cement becomes $8X_{21}$; the cost of shipping X_{22} truckloads of cement becomes $20X_{22}$, and, finally, the cost of shipping X_{23} truckloads of cement becomes $33X_{23}$. Once all of these elements are abstracted, the problem can be formulated. It is a "minimization" problem because the objective is to *minimize* the total transportation cost. That minimum will be expressed as Z in the formula below.

$$Z = 16X_{11} + 25X_{12} + 13X_{13} + 8X_{21} + 20X_{22} + 33X_{23}$$

Linear-programming techniques involving summing and some mathematical "tableaus" will be employed to find the minimum of this equation. The lessons for the cement company (and for you) are: 1) there *is* a solution to this problem, that is, a least-cost way of distributing the cement, given the constraints mentioned earlier; and 2) there would be no way to find that least-cost solution without mathematics.

The Federal Express Solution

In certain industries, distribution is not a secondary function but the primary one, as it is with United Parcel Service and Federal Express.

Frederick Smith, the founder of Federal Express, which guarantees next-day delivery service of packages and letters almost anywhere in the United States, tackled the problem of postal delivery while still an undergraduate at Yale University in the 1960s. He wrote a paper for an economics course proposing that if a postal service did not try to ship from point to point but rather, using a large fleet of planes and trucks, delivered every item during the night to one central location, then all incoming items could be sorted and shipped out to all delivery locations without having to determine efficiencies between local points. (It is said that he received a failing grade for the paper because his plan was too "unrealistic.")

Smith came from a wealthy family and when he had access to his inheritance he built a business based on his earlier idea. Today, 60 jet planes arrive at Memphis International Airport every night carrying parcels and mail that are sorted and reloaded on the same jets that take off again between 3 and 4 a.m. Computers track the location of each parcel and its destination (there can be as many as 500,000 pieces of mail in one night) and on-time delivery is attained in 99 percent of all cases.

Solving an Inventory Problem

Production and distribution are often linked to the problem of inventory size. Inventory is the stock of products for sale. The owner or the store manager has to keep enough of the product on hand to meet customers' needs. But the larger the inventory, the more money has to be spent on purchasing and storing the product, which ties up money the owner or manager could have invested elsewhere. Worse yet, items that are held too long in inventory may become stale or go out of style.

Inventory decisions can affect profits in a big way. Say the product costs $10 a piece wholesale and sells for $14. The markup is $4, so every missed sale is a loss of $4 in gross profit, but, at the same time, every item in the inventory represents an investment of an additional $10. For this reason, experienced merchandise managers make it their business to know how much to buy in order to have enough stock to cover *expected* sales, but not too much to burden the storage space or tie up too much working capital.

If demand is constant, the problem can be diagrammed in a fairly simple graph. In Figure 80, the expected demand is met during each time period by a delivery of quantity Q. During a normal sales period, the quantity on hand starts with Q and goes to zero, diminishing at a constant rate. This reduction of quantity is represented by a straight line because the relationship between quantity on hand and time is constant. When supplies are getting low, i.e., when the solid line representing the number on hand falls below the level R indicated by the horizontal broken line, management reorders the same quantity Q, and the same pattern is repeated.

Figure 80

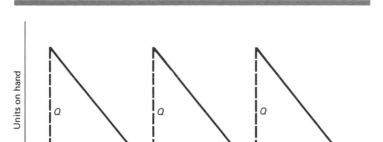

Time

This graph represents the outcome of a decision to order in quantities of Q on a regular basis. But if demand is fluctuating, how does a business choose that quantity Q? As we have just seen, storage costs are proportional to the amount stored. Ordering also entails a cost that will be proportional to the number of orders placed in a year. Now suppose the cost of placing an order suddenly increases compared to the cost of storage. Then, it might be a wiser business decision not to order quantity Q at the beginning of each time period, but, rather, to order less often and store greater quantities of the product, thereby cutting back on ordering costs as much as possible. Or, suppose that because of the size or fragility of the merchandise, it is more costly (and/or more risky) to hold large supplies in storage. Then it would be wiser to keep a smaller quantity on hand and order frequently. In short, the *relationship* between holding costs and ordering costs is important. Mathematics can help describe that relationship and suggest ways of minimizing the costs that depend upon it. Let's see how.

To determine the optimum order size, the first thing management will probably ask for is information about the cost of storing, and the planner will submit that information in a form like Figure 81. This graph shows, not surprisingly, that the larger the order quantity (Q) the higher the storage (holding) costs, because more

Figure 81

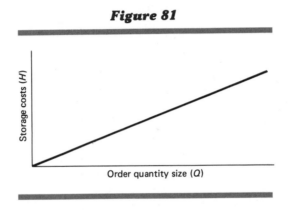

has to be stored longer. The average number of items on hand is one half of the order quantity (because it is a steady, that is, linear, decrease); therefore, where Q is the total quantity stored and H is the storage cost of one item, the algebraic expression for the cost of storing is

$$\frac{Q}{2} H$$

Next, management will want to have a comparable picture of the cost of placing orders. Out of the planning department will come a graph like Figure 82. As order quantity size (Q) goes up, the

Figure 82

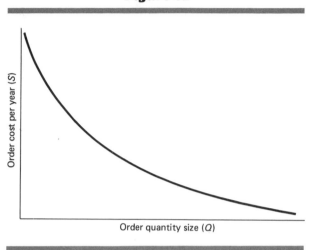

cost (S) of ordering per year will go down since fewer orders will have to be placed. This curve represents the algebraic expression

$$S = \frac{D}{Q} a$$

where

D = the annual quantity of merchandise

Q = the quantity of any one purchase order

S = the ordering cost for the year

a = the ordering cost per order regardless of size of order.

You can see that total holding costs go up as Q increases, while total ordering costs go down as Q increases. This is because the fewer orders, the less the business pays out in ordering costs, but the more it has to pay for storage.

At this point, management is ready to look at the data combined on a single graph to show total costs (Figure 83). DC (the annual purchase cost of merchandise, where C is the unit cost of merchandise) is represented on the graph by a horizontal line because, in

Figure 83

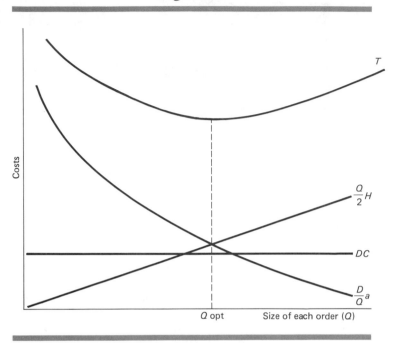

this instance, the cost of the merchandise is constant. No amount of wise decision making can alter that fact. But storage and ordering costs will go up and down as order quantity changes. Management is looking for an optimum order size (Q opt) that will provide least-cost stocking of goods. The top curve (T = total cost) is a sum of all the cost curves below. This is expressed algebraically as

$$T = DC + \frac{D}{Q}a + \frac{Q}{2}H.$$

The lowest point of the T curve is precisely the point that management is looking for: the optimal quantity size to order.

Once the elements in the problem are understood and translated into mathematical expressions, the laying out of the cost curves can be done and the minimum point on the total cost curve identified. The next step is to find the value of Q that minimizes the algebraic expression above; that is, to find the optimum ordering quantity (Q

opt) to maintain an adequate inventory at the lowest possible cost. This could be done by means of algebra, but it would be a tedious process. The most convenient method of solving this problem is with calculus.

Fluctuating Demand

What if demand is uncertain? Sometimes sales will be more than usual, so there always has to be a little extra inventory to cover that possibility. But how much extra? And when, in calculating the benefits and costs of a larger inventory, does it make sense *not* to order more?

Here is where the mathematics of probability enters the picture. A retailer (or manufacturer) has some historical data about the *range* of expected sales. This can be plotted on a monthly or annual graph. But to create a realistic inventory that would cover the highs and lows of demand, the planner may want to include a variety of different levels of demand and then assign probabilities to them, such as:

- 10 percent probability that sales will be 15 gross
- 20 percent probability that sales will be 35 gross
- 30 percent probability that sales will be 75 gross
- 20 percent probability that sales will be 90 gross
- 20 percent probability that sales will be 120 gross

The sum of the percentages has to total 100 percent.

Even with a range of figures for expected sales, based on history and some seasonal variation, the manager may still want to know specifically what the cost will be of maintaining more inventory than necessary compared with the cost of lost sales because of too little inventory. Modeling can help answer this question as well.

One way to research the inventory problem is to *simulate* what would happen over a relatively long period of time (say 120 months) if one or another ordering strategy were used. To do this, management will ask a computer specialist to set up a program to do simulation runs of orders based on various sets of assumptions and strategies. By this means, the effect of one strategy over another can be compared and the strategy that maximizes overall profit in the simulation will then be tried in the real world.

Peggy's Inventory Simulation

Peggy Beranek is a student of management information systems. She did her undergraduate work in Spanish and computer science with a strong minor in mathematics. She followed this with a master's degree in business (MBA) and is now studying for a Ph.D. in management information systems. Peggy's task is to help a retailer decide which of eight possible ordering strategies to use with regard to one expensive item he stocks. He wants to have enough on hand to meet expected orders, but not too much to burden the storage capacity of the business or to tie up too much capital.

After interviewing the retailer, Peggy learns that he likes to buy this item infrequently and in bulk because there is a high cost involved in ordering the product. In addition to shipping costs of $12 per gross, there is an ordering expense (to cover paper work and billing) each time of $200. So, the retailer has to be cautious about ordering too often. Meanwhile, demand for the item is very volatile. He can sell as few as 15 gross in one month and sometimes as many as 120 gross. In addition to ordering costs, Peggy will also have to consider storage costs at $5 per month per gross. So, while the retailer doesn't want to order too frequently, he also doesn't want to order too much, lest he incur a high inventory expense. On the other hand, if his stock runs low, he has to special order for his customers, which costs an additional $6 per gross in handling charges. Given these various costs, how can the retailer find out what the best ordering strategy is for the firm?

One way is to pick one ordering strategy (say 90 gross per month ordered once a month) and conduct business on a seesaw, overinventorying or missing sales. Another is to try one ordering strategy for a six-month period and then another for the next six. But, that way, one would never know whether an ordering strategy succeeded by accident or because it was really the best. A third approach is to *simulate* buying and selling that particular product over 10 full years of doing business. That way, the retailer could see how each of the eight different ordering strategies performed over time.

This third approach is accomplished by computer simulation. Peggy can construct a computer model that will try out a whole series of ordering strategies for the firm, report on the effect on profit of each, and then recommend to the owner which strategy to follow. If her assumptions are carefully drawn, and her demand fluctuations realistic, the computer's printout can accurately project—without one item actually arriving or leaving inventory—what the costs and profit will be over a 10-year period.

The Model

Peggy wants to create a model that will test each of the retailer's ordering strategies through a complete 120-month cycle of possible orders. In each stage, the program will simulate the arrival of goods from the supplier, the demand for goods from the retailer's customers, and whether an order has to be placed. Every regular order costs $200 plus $12 per gross. Every special order is charged an additional $6 per gross. Finally, for every gross of items held in inventory there will be a charge of $5 per gross per month. These are the constraints, called the *parameters* of the problem.

Now, how will Peggy simulate the most likely demand over time? She will build in several different demands and a percentage probability for each, so that as the simulation proceeds, the computer can keep shifting demands in order to simulate a wide range of reasonable possibilities that might occur in the real world. Here is how she describes the range of demand that might occur in any given month at any time during that month:

- 10 percent probability that sales will be 15 gross
- 20 percent probability that sales will be 35 gross
- 30 percent probability that sales will be 75 gross
- 20 percent probability that sales will be 90 gross
- 20 percent probability that sales will be 120 gross

Her task is to test eight ordering strategies based on four different totals (60, 70, 80, and 90 gross per month), each ordered either once in bulk or in half-lots twice a month. Spelled out, the eight possibilities are

Order Size ×	30	60	35	70	40	80	45	90
Order Interval	2	1	2	1	2	1	2	1
Total Order Per Month	60	60	70	70	80	80	90	90

There are three different kinds of "events" that will occur during the run of the model:

- The placing of an order for goods
- The arrival of goods to the system
- The demand (sales) of goods

When each of these events occurs, inventory will be updated appropriately. For example, when goods arrive, inventory will increase by that amount; when sales take place, inventory will decrease. The placing of an order will set a process in motion that will soon cause goods to arrive, but will itself not change inventory.

Finally, costs will be calculated by a cost-calculator in the program; storage costs on a per-item basis each month, ordering costs for regular and special orders, and an annual profit will be computed.

The Flowchart

The second thing a researcher does after getting to know the nature of the problem and before writing the computer program is to set up a flowchart. A flowchart is a kind of outline of the flow of logic that will drive the model. Each computer programmer has his or her own style of writing the flowchart. But there are some standard "shapes" that most people use to remind themselves of the three stages of the process: information gathering or dissemination is expressed in the form of parallelograms; processing the information or simple calculations are in the form of rectangles; and decisions to be made are in the form of diamonds.

In order for programmers to concentrate on the general outline of the problem, a whole series of processes, decisions, or other actions can be enclosed in a rectangle with extra lines along the sides. This enclosing process is called a subroutine. Each subroutine will also have its own flowchart. By enclosing small details inside a subroutine, the programmer can focus on the logic necessary to solve the particular problem.

At first glance a typical flowchart resembles a kind of treasure map or children's game (see Figure 84). On Peggy's flowchart the first box after *start* has to do with setting a series of "clocks" in motion that will keep count of the events and of their corresponding

Figure 84

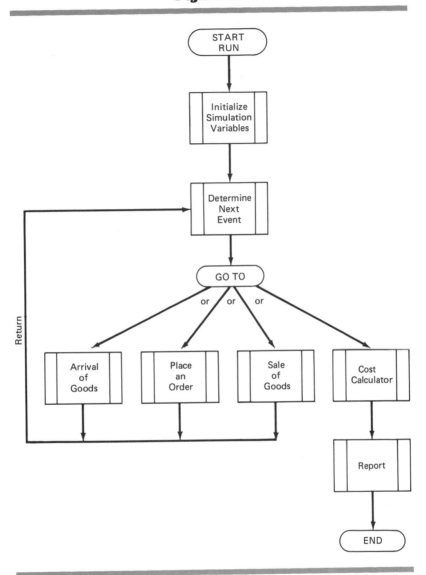

costs as these occur. This step is called the *initializing* step. Here is where the *parameters*—the given costs—are entered in: the $5 per gross per month storage cost; the $12 per gross shipping cost; the $200 expense per order, and so on, making the run as realistic as possible. Here, too, is where the particular inventory and ordering strategies would be determined. For instance, the inventory might be set for 80 gross if Peggy decides to begin each run with 80 items in stock. If she wanted to begin with an ordering strategy of 35 gross per two-week period, this would be entered in at this point, too. The initializing process is very important because it is these strategies that are to be *simulated* in the progam run.

The *next event* is where some randomness occurs. Think of this as the wheel spinning in a board game. The "needle" could just as well land on *arrival of goods, place an order,* or *sale of goods*— and in any sequence. Moreover, just as it would in real life, the quantity of any particular *sale of goods* will vary randomly within a certain range. There are some subroutines within the *next event* section of the flowchart. (Vertical lines at the ends of the boxes always indicate subroutines.) That is because *next events* are not entirely random. When there is a sudden *sale of goods* under conditions of inadequate inventory, an order will have to be placed whether it is due to be placed or not, and the ordering cost penalty paid. Similarly, costs will have to be continually entered into the *cost calculator* for storage, for ordering, and for shipment as these costs are incurred. So the *next event* portion of the program is in many ways its driving force.

The *go to* step, in contrast, is best thought of as a traffic director. Depending on what *next event* comes up in the earlier step, the program will register either an arrival of goods, a new order, or some amount of sales based on a randomized sequence of demand for goods. After any event, the *go to* step will direct the inventory to be updated and the costs transferred to the *cost calculator*. Eventually, after 120 months of events and responses have been simulated, the costs are tallied into a final report. Then the program is entirely rerun to test each of the remaining seven ordering strategies.

Suppose, in the course of a run, the *next event* turns out to be a certain sale of goods. The program will then check to see whether that demand can be met by goods in stock. If there are enough, the program will simply register the sale and deduct that quantity of goods from inventory. If there are not enough in stock, the program will return to *next event* and specify that the next event be *placing an order* in a certain quantity. This, in turn, will trigger the cost calculator and, after a predictable time, the arrival of a new order. The arrival of the new order, in turn, changes the total number of goods in stock and signals the cost calculator to start adding up storage costs. Then the next random event occurs.

Every time the program returns to the *next event* determinator, it notes the completion of some sort of transaction; and when a "month" of such transactions has passed (however the passage of time is clocked in the program), another "month" of events begins. Only after 120 months have elapsed (perhaps no more than 2 minutes in actual time) will Peggy's program have fully tested one ordering strategy. Before beginning another 120-month run, she would re-initialize the simulation variables to try strategy 2.

While much of the detail of computer simulation does not appear in this example of a flowchart—the actual program written in Pascal or Fortran would be 10 pages in length—the key parts are covered in these few boxes and lines. With a flowchart in hand Peggy can write the program so that the computer can do the tedious simulation of 10 years times 8 ordering strategies at 5 shifting demands in just minutes of computer time.

Choosing a Programming Language

The next task, after setting up a flowchart, is choosing a computer language. Ideally the programmer will choose a language that matches the type of problem. COBOL is usually used for business problems, FORTRAN and Pascal for scientific ones, PL/1 for either type, and many other languages for very special applications. Each language has its own syntax or rules of grammar that structures how the problem is actually written. Other factors affecting language selection are the size of the computer and the programmer's own background knowledge.

When Peggy has written a computer program based on her flowchart, she is ready to run her simulation on the computer, which will give her a full picture of what happens to profit with each of the eight ordering strategies. If the inputs she was given were correct and she has done her work carefully, she should be able to give her client sound guidelines for the most profitable ordering strategy.

Planning Your Own Strategy

Much of the quantitative analysis used in business today is being done on the computer. But planners don't have to do their own programming anymore. Entire ready-made programs are now available for purchase that do the hard work—payroll packages, linear-programming packages, simulation packages, data-base and spreadsheet packages. The business planner only has to feed in the right numbers to adapt a program to the needs of a particular firm. But the user of these packages still has to understand the mathematics behind them in order to know what is going on. Once the computer has run its course, the results are pages of numbers. If you don't know what those numbers mean, you won't be able to make a valid decision.

Hence, a good strategy for a student who wants a career in business is to take courses in "finite mathematics," calculus, quantitative methods, statistics, probability, and computer programming. With these skills and a general familiarity with the power of mathematical applications, you will be very well prepared to think precisely and creatively about solving the kinds of problems business decisions entail.

Chapter

10

Getting Comfortable with Math

People who are comfortable with mathematics perceive the world in ways that are not available to people who are not. They see connections between quantities the way students of history perceive connections between events. They grasp the essentials of a problem and can abstract these by means of notation so as to be able to predict—without going through a large number of calculations—what will happen if any of those essentials were to change. They have a sense of what is "absolute" and what is "relative" in a particular context. They understand that to say an object is "moving slowly" has little meaning, except in relation to something else. And they are unlikely to be fooled by statements that don't hold up to quantitative analysis. They know that to say "the inflation rate is going down," does not mean that inflation itself is going down; rather, only that the rate of *increase* is diminishing, or, more visually, that on a graph showing price against time the curve is flattening out.

People who are comfortable with mathematics are not limited to using vaguely defined terms like fast or slow, or more or less. They can reformulate definitions and problems in such a way that

235

numbers can be attached to them. Speed becomes distance over time. Power becomes energy over time. Doubling time is expressed in terms of a certain rate of growth. Such people are able to make decisions that are more precise because they understand the relationship between quantities.

How will you know when you are getting comfortable with mathematics? You might find yourself paying closer attention to the numbers and quantities around you, recalling them with greater ease, and thinking harder and more creatively about them. You will start noticing that quantities very often exist in mathematical relationships and that much mathematical insight resides in those relationships. Once you realize that relationships are often much clearer when displayed visually on graphs, you will start sketching graphs yourself. Graphing equations is not just an exercise in a mathematics class. It is a precise and powerful way of conveying complex information, information that can only awkwardly be rendered in words.

While we students of mathematics have to work within our written and spoken language, we also, slowly, have to think about liberating ourselves from the language we know and getting used to thinking in notation and in graphic images. Speaking that new language out loud is one good way to become more fluent. And it is for this reason that I have indicated how to say mathematical expressions like Δt (delta t), chi-square, or

$$\frac{A^i e^{-A}}{i!}$$

(A raised to the ith power times e raised to the minus A power divided by i factorial). But the words are just temporary supports until a mathematical understanding of notation and graphic relationships is soundly in place.

A recently released report attempted to explain the poor performance of American students on international mathematics tests. The report included not just test scores but results of interviews with Asian and American parents, teachers, and teenagers, and out of these interviews comes an important qualitative insight. It appears that Asians think of mathematics "ability" as fairly equally distributed among individuals and that differences in mathematical performance are the result of hard work. Americans apparently believe the opposite: that mathematical ability is a very rare talent, possessed by only a few and utterly impossible to attain if one is not born with a gift for it; hard work, then, has little to do with increasing mathematical understanding. And, with this perception, American teenagers continue to sink below their international peers in mathematical performance.

Suppose Asians are right and that mathematical ability is nothing more than *study, persistence,* and *hard work.* This is not a theorem that can be proved or disproved. But it could be a point of departure for your new beginning in mathematics. There would then be no need to worry either about math ability, math inability, or even math disability. All you would need is confidence, time, and some appetite for the work that lies ahead.

Further Reading

Reading *about* mathematics is no substitute for *doing* mathematics, but since you have come this far, you clearly enjoy reading and might want to consult some other books that enlarge on and continue the ideas explored in this book. The following list is by no means comprehensive. Most of the books are in print. Those marked with an asterisk are not, and therefore will be available only in libraries. Do some browsing on your own in the mathematics section of your school or public library.

Mathematics: History and More

Asimov, Isaac. *Asimov on Numbers*. New York: Pocket Books, 1977. Isaac Asimov, one of the most widely published popular science writers, selected these essays on mathematics from his regular columns. All the author's talents for clarifying and explaining as well as entertaining are brought to bear on a most interesting set of topics.

Bell, E. T. *Men of Mathematics*. New York: Simon and Schuster, 1937. This is a mathematics classic. Bell traces the history of mathematics through the intriguing lives and personalities of great mathematicians. A supplement—the story of some of the world's great women mathematicians—can be found in *Terri Perl's *Math Equals* (Menlo Park, Calif.: Addison Wesley, 1978).

Dantzig, Tobias. *Numbers: The Language of Science*. New York: Free Press, 1954. This book is my personal favorite: a readable and understandable "tour" of mathematics, both historical and topical. In it are discussions in much greater depth of many of the topics treated in *Succeed with Math,* such as the search for the "last number" and the history of the discovery of multiple infinities, to cite but two examples.

Hersh, Reuben, and Philip J. Davis. *The Mathematical Experience*. Boston: Houghton Mifflin, 1981. This is a broad introduction to what *doing* mathematics is all about. Some sections are more difficult than others, but all are worth dipping into for insight into how mathematicians think and what they think about. This book is especially useful because of its nontechnical treatment

238

of mathematics in traditionally mathematics-free disciplines such as sociology, psychology, medicine, and linguistics.

Hogben, Lancelot. *Mathematics for the Millions.* New York: Pocket Books, 1965. A classic history of and general introduction to mathematics—perhaps the most popular book of its kind. You will find Hogben's treatment of probability and statistics particularly useful.

Eves, Howard. *An Introduction to the History of Mathematics.* New York: Holt, Rinehart & Winston, 1969. This is a basic book for nonspecialists. Also look at his newer work, *Great Moments in Mathematics,* Vols. I and II (Washington, D.C.: Mathematical Association of America, 1980 and 1981).

Guillen, Michael. *Bridges to Infinity: The Human Side of Mathematics.* Los Angeles: Jeremy Tarcher, 1983. The author gives you a look at what mathematicians find interesting in their work.

Kline, Morris. *Mathematics for the Nonmathematician.* New York: Dover, 1967. This is a classic in the field. Also look at his newer book, *Mathematics: The Loss of Certainty* (New York: Oxford, 1980), which deals with the fallibility of mathematics and mathematicians as well as the philosophy and foundations of mathematics.

Mathematics Reference

Standard encyclopedias remain—as in all fields—excellent sources of historical and substantive information about topics in mathematics. The articles are written for nonspecialists by experts.

Shapiro, Max S., ed. *Mathematics Encyclopedia: A Made-Simple Book.* New York: Doubleday, 1977. You cannot learn mathematics by reading an encyclopedia any more than you can learn a foreign language by reading a dictionary. Still, it is useful to have a collection of mathematical facts, tables, formulas, and definitions in one compact volume—and in alphabetical order. There are other, more comprehensive mathematical encyclopedias, but this one will do for the beginning college student.

Unusual (College Level) Texts

Mathematics texts are weighty and expensive, so you are not likely to purchase more than are necessary. Still, it is wise to look at others in the library both because other authors may be more attuned to your questions and problems, and because it is useful to remind yourself that there is more than one way to state and explain a problem. Following are a few unusual texts in college-level mathematics that might interest you.

Campbell, Douglas M. *The Whole Craft of Numbers*. Boston: Prindle, Weber & Schmid, 1977. This is a fine text that combines history, topics in mathematics, puzzles, problems, and practice methods, and is written to stimulate as well as to teach and entertain.

Driver, R. D. *Why Math?* New York: Springer-Verlag, 1984. This excellent alternate approach to college-level mathematics is rich in applications.

Hilton, Peter, and Jean Pedersen. *Fear No More: An Adult Approach to Mathematics*. Menlo Park, California: Addison Wesley, 1983. This well-written "reintroduction" to arithmetic is by two eminent mathematicians, one an algebraist, the other a geometer. The subject is familiar but the treatment is innovative. Hilton and Petersen have strong ideas about what should (and should not) be taught in elementary school, and how it should be taught. Anyone who follows their reasoning will never again be confused by fractions or negative numbers. This is the first of three proposed volumes (the second on algebra, the third on calculus).

Jacobs, Harold R. *Mathematics: A Human Endeavor*. San Francisco: W. H. Freeman, 1970. The author describes this as "a textbook for those who think they don't like the subject." It is a very highly regarded introduction and review of important topics in mathematics—a sophisticated verbal and conceptual treatment that does not presume any prior mastery of mathematics. Perfect for the nonmajor.

Stein, Sherman K. *Mathematics: The Man-Made Universe*. San Francisco: W. H. Freeman, 1963. This is one of several texts prepared for "liberal arts students," and is therefore freer in its sequence, richer in its prose, and larded with interesting tidbits and applications.

Chapter-Related Suggestions

Chapter 1: Making Math Work for You
Brush, Lorelei R. *Encouraging Girls in Mathematics: The Problem and the Solution*. Cambridge, Mass.: Abt Books, 1980. In the

1970s certain myths about "girls and mathematics" began to crumble, thanks to the research of psychologists and mathematics educators such as Lorelei Brush. This book is a scholarly treatment of the subject based on Dr. Brush's research, but it also includes suggestions for change.

Tobias, Sheila. *Overcoming Math Anxiety.* Boston: Houghton Mifflin, 1980. This book, intended for adults who had long ago given up on themselves and mathematics, discusses "math avoidance," "mathematics and sex," and "right and wrong-headedness," and also explores arithmetic ("everyday math"), calculus ("Sunday math"), and techniques for overcoming math anxiety.

Turner, Nura D. *Mathematics and My Career.* Washington, D. C.: National Council of Teachers of Mathematics, 1971. This book is just one of many publications of the NCTM and the Mathematical Association of America designed to inform students of the many uses of mathematics in today's world. This particular collection is notable in that the several authors (including a musician and a clergyman) write about their personal encounters with mathematics and how their ability to do mathematics has served them professionally. Other NCTM or MAA publications are in libraries or can be ordered from the organizations.

Chapter 2: Reading Math

While there are no books I know of on "reading" mathematics, it is a subject for scholarly research. Additional insights can be found in certain sections of the following:

Maxwell, E. A. *Fallacies in Mathematics.* Cambridge: Cambridge University Press, 1959. This book points out certain not-very-obvious fallacies in the history of mathematics in an effort to teach readers to notice what is *wrong* with an argument and how to improve critical reading and reasoning skills.

Solow, Daniel. *How to Read and Do Proofs.* New York: Wiley, 1982. This introduction to the mathematical thought process focuses on proofs but offers some important lessons in "reading" mathematics in general.

Chapter 3: Problem Solving

Brown, Stephen I., and Marion I. Walter. *The Art of Problem Posing.* Philadelphia: Franklin Institute, 1983. By focusing on posing problems, the authors describe a series of activities students can do while struggling to solve a problem.

Davis, G. A. *Psychology of Problem-Solving*. New York: Basic Books, 1973. This is a more abstract discussion of the art of problem solving.

Polya, G. *How to Solve It*. Princeton: Princeton University Press, 1973. First written in 1944, this book has become a classic in the subject of problem solving. Its strength is its codification of useful problem-solving strategies without discouraging flexible approaches involving the imagination and trial-and-error. A must.

Whimbey, Arthur, and Jack Lochhead. *Problem Solving and Comprehension: A Short Course in Analytical Reasoning*. Philadelphia: Franklin Institute, 1980. Here is another contribution to the theory and practice of problem solving that provides workbook-like activities you can do on your own as well as a treatment of the kind of analytic reasoning skills that will contribute to success in reading and thinking systematically about difficult textual material. Chapter 5, "Six Myths about Reading," provides a list of "don'ts" that complements Chapter 2 in *Succeed with Math*.

Chapter 4: The Wonders of Pi

Beckmann, Petr. *The History of Pi*. New York: St. Martin's, 1971. Like myself, Beckmann finds much interesting history and many important mathematical ideas linked to the concept of pi. His treatment is far more extensive, and in some chapters more difficult, than mine, but if you have become addicted to pi, this book should be on your list.

Sawyer, W. W. *What Is the Calculus About?* New York: Random House, 1971. Sawyer is a much-admired mathematician and teacher of mathematics. In this excellent short book, he provides the overview and the logic of the subject of calculus that you might want to look at before taking the subject. Like me, he begins with speed and other everyday applications of the smooth curve of change.

Steinhaus, H. *Mathematical Snapshots*. New York: Oxford, 1969. Steinhaus considers mathematics concerned with real-world applications to nature and physics.

Weyl, H. *Symmetry*. Princeton: Princeton University Press. Weyl is considered one of the greatest mathematicians of this century. In this book he examines symmetry as it occurs in art and nature and includes some beautiful photographs.

Chapter 5: Taming Numbers

Davis, P. J. *The Lore of Large Numbers*. Washington, D.C.: Mathematical Association of America, 1961. Through an exposition of computation, estimation, and approximation, Davis familiarizes his reader with notions of pi, exponents, scientific notation, and infinite sequences in a way to spark general interest.

*Reid, Constance. *From Zero to Infinity: What Makes Numbers Interesting?* New York: Crowell, 1960. Using the numbers from zero through nine and then infinity as her table of contents, the author covers much in the history and theory of numbers as theory evolved over the centuries.

Chapter 6: Equalities and Inequalities

Chvatal, Vasek. *Linear Programming*. New York: W. H. Freeman, 1983. This textbook is hard going for the beginner but is worth consulting when you get into the subject in your courses.

Feiring, Bruce. *Linear Programming: An Introduction*. New York: Sage, 1986. I haven't been able to locate general introductions to linear programming, but this, though a text, is highly recommended.

*Harish, Verma, and Charles W. Gross. *Introduction to Quantitative Methods: A Managerial Approach*. New York: John Wiley, 1978. Chapter 5 provides an introduction to linear programming techniques.

Chapter 7: Social Science

Olnik, M. *An Introduction to Mathematical Models in Social and Life Sciences*. Reading, Mass.: Addison Wesley, 1978. This book, although a bit difficult, covers issues raised in both Chapters 7 and 8.

Wallace, Walter L. *The Logic of Science in Sociology*. Chicago: Aldine-Atherton, 1971. This is an abstract treatment of the methods used in social-science research covering measurement, sampling, hypotheses generating, and the interpretation of data.

Chapter 8: Biology

The three books listed below tell the story of the development of modern biology in the nineteenth and twentieth centuries. Coleman's deals primarily with nineteenth-century developments, Allen's with twentieth-century developments; Eiseley's book is a classic survey of Darwinianism and evolution.

Allen, Graham. *Life Science in the Twentieth Century*. New York: John Wiley and Sons, 1975.

Coleman, William. *Biology in the Nineteenth Century*. New York: John Wiley and Sons, 1971.

Eiseley, Loren. *Darwin's Century*. New York: Doubleday-Anchor Books, 1958.

Chapter 9: Economics and Business

Deane, Phyllis. *The Evolution of Economic Ideas*. Cambridge: Cambridge University Press, 1978. This is my choice of a concise yet comprehensive history of economics for both the beginning economics student and the student who just wants to know how modern economics came into being.

Mathematics in the Modern World: Readings from Scientific American. San Francisco: W. H. Freeman, 1968. Of particular interest is Part V, which treats (among other topics) mathematics in the social, biological, and business sciences.

Miller, D. W., and M. K. Starr. *The Structure of Human Decisions*. Englewood Cliffs, N.J.: Prentice Hall, 1967. This book includes three chapters on decision theory, which bear on the economics and business applications touched on in Chapter 9.

Hopper, Grace, and Steven Mandell. *Understanding Computers*. St. Paul, Minn.: West, 1986. Grace Hopper is a retired navy captain who began working on the Mark I, one of the first computers ever manufactured; helped develop the first "compiler," the technique for translating a programming language into a language the machine could understand; and standardized the basic business computer programming language of COBOL. This book is a good introduction to the nature and uses of computers.

Graham, Neill. *The Mind Tool: Computers and Their Impact on Society*. St. Paul, Minn.: West, 1986. This is a good book for the person who knows very little about computers.

Sanders, Jo S., and Antonia Stone. *Neuter Computer: Computers for Girls & Boys*. New York: Neal-Schuman, 1986. This book is a critique of the false notion that there is something "masculine" about computers and computer use; it's a good general introduction to computing.

Trainor, Timothy. *Computer Literacy: Concepts and Applications*. Santa Cruz, Calif.: Mitchell, 1984. Written for the high school and early college student.

Fun and Games

Mathematics *is* fun, but not until you get the subject under your control and stop feeling anxious about it. No list of recommended readings in mathematics would be complete without some mention of the work of two mathematician-writers who regularly contribute columns to *Scientific American*. One is Martin Gardner, whose puzzles, games, and intriguing problems have been collected and published in numerous books, such as *Wheels, Life, and Other Mathematical Amusement* (New York: W. H. Freeman, 1983). The other is A. K. Dewdney, whose puzzles tend to have more to do with computers. Dewdney has published a collection called *The Plainverse: Computer Contact with a Two-Dimensional World* (New York: Poseidon, 1984). It is written for the kind of person who reads *Scientific American* with understanding and pleasure. Once you are comfortable with mathematics you may find these "mind games" instructive as well as amusing. An easier place to start may be with James Fixx's books (not the James Fixx of "running" fame): *Games for the Super Intelligent* (1982), *More Games for the Super Intelligent* (1982), and *Solve It* (1983), all published by Warner Books.

Index

Abedon, Stephen T., 182, 189–99
acceleration, 71–76
aleph (ℵ), 68
algebra, 113–14
  geometry and, 116–20
  inequalities in, 114–16
  linear programming and, 133–34, 142
  for problem solving, 41–44
  variables in, 114–15
Allen, Graham, 180
anxiety from mathematics, 4–11
approximating numbers, 110–11
Archimedes, 79–80
area of circles, 76–80
arithmetic sequences, 102
  summing, 106–10
artificial selection, 181
Asians, attitudes toward mathematics
  among, 236–37
averages
  variation around the mean in, 163–64
  weighted, 196
Avogadro, Amadeo, 101
Avogadro's number, 101–2
axes, 116
  in Cartesian coordinates, 119–20
  in economics, 210
  on graphs, 28–29

Babylonia, ancient, 63
Bach, Johann Sebastian, 92
bacteria, 190–91
Beckmann, Petr, 63
Beranek, Peggy, 228–29
Bernstein, Harris, 189–91
binary numbers, 96
biology
  mathematics used in, 179–83
  Mendel's work in, 183–85
  microbiological experiments in, 190–99
  of population genetics, 185–89

bits (binary digits), 96
blacks, discrimination against, 5
braking speeds, 93–94
brightness of light, 94–96
budget lines, 207
bushel problem, 37–47
business
  inventory problems in, 222–23
  mathematics used in, 216–22
  strategic planning in, 234
  see also economics
bytes, 96

calculus
  invention of, 80
  as prerequisite to statistics and probability, 176
  used in economics, 204–9
Cantor, Georg, 12
Cartesian coordinates, 119–20
  equalities graphed on, 120–26
  inequalities graphed on, 126–28
change
  acceleration as, 71–76
  continuous, 70–71
chemistry, Avogadro's number in, 101–2
chi square test (χ^2), 168–75
circles
  in derivations of pi, 60–62
  pi and, 57–60
  pi to determine area of, 76–80
clavier (musical instrument), 92
COBOL (programming language), 233
computers
  powers of 2 used in, 96
  programming languages for, 233
  and random numbers, 157
  used for business decisions, 234
confidence levels, in sample selection, 162

246

Other Books of Interest from the College Board

Item #

002601   *Campus Visits and College Interviews,* by Zola Dincin Schneider. An "insider's" guide to campus visits and college interviews, including 12 checklists that will help students make the most of these firsthand opportunities. ISBN: 0-87447-260-1, $9.95

002261   *The College Admissions Organizer.* This unique planning tool for college-bound students includes inserts and fill-in forms, plus 12 large pockets to store important admissions materials. ISBN: 0-87447-226-1, $16.95

002687   *The College Board Achievement Tests.* Complete and actual Achievement Tests given in 13 subjects, plus the College Board's official advice on taking the tests. ISBN: 0-87447-268-7, $9.95

003101   *The College Board Guide to Preparing for the PSAT/NMSQT.* Contains four actual tests as well as practical test-taking tips, sample questions, and a comprehensive math review section. ISBN: 0-87447-310-1, $8.95

002938   *The College Board Guide to the CLEP Examinations.* Contains nearly 900 questions from CLEP general and subject examinations, plus other information. ISBN: 0-87447-293-8, $8.95

003047   *College Bound: The Student's Handbook for Getting Ready, Moving In, and Succeeding on Campus,* by Evelyn Kaye and Janet Gardner. Help for high school seniors as they face the responsibilities and independence of being college freshmen. ISBN: 0-87447-304-7, $9.95

003152   *The College Cost Book, 1988–89.* A step-by-step guide to 1988–89 college costs and detailed financial aid for 3,100 accredited institutions. ISBN: 0-87447-315-2, $12.95 (Updated annually)

003160   *The College Guide for Parents,* by Charles J. Shields. Useful information on such topics as college choice, standardized testing, college applications, financial aid, and coping with separation anxiety. ISBN: 0-87447-316-0, $12.95

003136   *The College Handbook, 1988–89.* The College Board's official directory to more than 3,100 two- and four-year colleges and universities. ISBN: 0-87447-313-6, $16.95 (Updated annually)

002490   *College to Career,* by Joyce Slayton Mitchell. A guide to more than 100 careers, telling what the work is like, the education and personal skills needed, how many people are employed, where they work, and starting salaries and future employment prospects. ISBN: 0-87447-249-0, $9.95

003055   *How to Help Your Teenager Find the Right Career,* by Charles J. Shields. Step-by-step advice and innovative ideas to help parents motivate their children to explore careers and find alternatives suited to their interests and abilities. ISBN: 0-87447-305-5, $12.95

002482   *How to Pay for Your Children's College Education,* by Gerald Krefetz. Practical advice to help parents of high school students, as well as of young children, finance their children's college education. ISBN: 0-87447-248-2, $12.95

003144   *Index of Majors, 1988–89.* Lists 500 majors at the 3,000 colleges and graduate institutions, state by state, that offer them. ISBN: 0-87447-314-4, $13.95 (Updated annually)

         Profiles in Achievement, by Charles M. Holloway. Traces the careers of eight outstanding men and women who used education as the key to later success.

002911   Hardcover   ISBN: 0-87447-291-1, $15.95
002857   Paperback   ISBN: 0-87447-285-7, $9.95

003039   *10 SATs: Third Edition.* Ten actual, recently administered SATs plus the full text of *Taking the SAT,* the College Board's official advice. ISBN: 0-87447-303-9, $9.95

002571   *Writing Your College Application Essay,* by Sarah Myers McGinty. An informative and reassuring book that helps students write distinctive application essays and explains what colleges are looking for in these essays. ISBN: 0-87447-257-1, $9.95

002474   *Your College Application,* by Scott Gelband, Catherine Kubale, and Eric Schorr. A step-by-step guide to help students do their best on college applications. ISBN: 0-87447-247-4, $9.95

To order by direct mail any books not available in your local bookstore, please specify the item number and send your request with a check made payable to the College Board for the full amount to: College Board Publications, Department M53, Box 886, New York, New York 10101-0886. Allow 30 days for delivery. An institutional purchase order is required in order to be billed, and postage will be charged on all billed orders. Telephone orders are not accepted, but information regarding any of the above titles is available by calling Publications Customer Service at (212) 713-8165.